Conquer the Universe with Astrology

Love and Seduction by Starlight

Matthew Currie

Printed and bound in Canada.

ISBN#: 978-0-9865102-6-7

Theophania Publishing
Calgary Alberta Canada

ABOUT THIS BOOK

A book is more than merely the information contained within its covers; it is the experience of the reader combined with the presentation which makes the information a memorable experience. Octavia & Co. Press is a small press publisher specializing in unique, handcrafted books. Each book produced by Theophania Publishingis a work of art, intended to be cherished by its owners - even the most subtle design is crafted with elegance. We offer a variety of services to take your book idea from conception to market. Contact us for more information on how we can make your dream library become a reality.

For my Radha

"Although the effulgence of the moon is brilliant initially at night, in the daytime it fades away. Similarly, although the lotus is beautiful during the daytime, at night it closes. But, O My friend, the face of My most dear Srimati Radharani is always bright and beautiful, both day and night. Therefore, to what can Her face be compared?"

-Vidagdha-madhava 5.20

Introduction
What Lights Up Your Sky?

Whether most professional astrologers like it or not, most people (at least in Western Culture) get their first introduction to Astrology via Sun Signs. After all, it's the only factor in a birth chart than can immediately be determined by the birthday. Knowing one or two traits that go along with each Sun Sign can be a quick and easy way to get a handle on someone's personality. Of course, humans are a lot more complex than that and focusing on the Sun Sign can be a convenient way to shoehorn the infinite complexity of the personality into an easy-to-digest (or dismiss) package.

This sort of thing probably does as much harm as good, overall but it's certainly *convenient*.

Less convenient (unless you live in a culture with a lunar-based calendar) but equally important is the sign placement of The Moon. Let's be honest here: The Moon in the sky is a lot less showy than The Sun. It doesn't generate its own light – it only reflects sunshine. No plants rely on moonlight to photosynthesize. Current theory tends to indicate that The Moon was formed when a planetoid smacked into the still-forming Earth, and that The Moon is simply a congealed glob of what would have been the top layer of our planet. But the interesting thing is that if that had not happened life as we know it on Earth may not have been possible.

Think about that for a moment: The Sun is all showy and obvious like a person's Ego. But, honestly: if you've never kissed anyone in the moonlight, you may very well have missed the whole point of Life Itself. The Moon is smaller and far less concerned with how it looks than the Sun/Ego is like a person's basic Emotional Responses. You need *both* to be a real, fully developed person.

This book will help you understand the basic nature of the Sun and Moon in each sign. And, in one easy step, you will have expanded your astrological understanding of people from twelve basic types, to twelve *times* twelve *one hundred and forty-four* basic personality types.

Astrology, like life itself, is complex. Fortunately, it isn't too hard to get a basic handle on some of the details.

So what's all this got to do with "Love and Seduction"?

Of course, there's still more yet to it all. Once you've established who you are there is communication (Mercury), love and affection (Venus), and your drives, sexual and otherwise (Mars).

As an astrologer, the majority of consultations I do are centered on issues related to Love. And whether you planned it that way or not seduction is a part of the process, as surely as the salesman is a part of the process when you buy a car. Everyone, of course, likes to think they're above that. The very word "seduction" conjures images of users and bleary-eyed mornings of regret. And sure: sometimes that's what seduction ends with, just like there really *are* a few crooked car salesmen out there.

But the truth is that "salesmanship" is a part of life whenever you interact with someone new. No matter how qualified you may feel you are for a job, you still spell-check your résumé and dress nicely.

Most of the clients I have come to me with one of two major issues:

1. Where is the love that I really want/need?

2. Why is the love I have not working out the way I want it to?

And to be perfectly honest, more often than not the answer(s) to those questions boil down to two very simple factors:

1. You don't fully understand the assets you have, or you aren't using them properly
2. You don't *really* understand how your partner is wired.

This e-book will give you the tools you need to understand yourself, your moods, and how you interact with and love others. It will also give you the means to get a fully-formed handle on the people you love (or would like to love, or would like to have loving you).

Look up your own placements first, and see how those various pictures add up to make you who you are. If you have the birth data for anyone you have (or had) a relationship with (or unrequited love, or desire, or real contempt for) in past, look them up too. Before long, you'll find yourself saying "Why didn't I know this before! Think of all the time and trouble I could have saved myself!"

Also: the better you understand yourself and others using astrology, the more money you'll save on counsellors, bad dates and astrologers. You'll thank me later

Part One: The Sun - Your Big, Fat Ego

Even people who know nothing else about Astrology know what their "Sun Sign" is. There are two reasons for this. One is that the Sun Sign for most people is easily determined by their birthday. Secondly, the Sun in your astrological birth chart represents the Ego... and the Ego loves having birthday parties thrown for it, so naturally it remembers the date. People don't usually say "I have Sun in Leo," they say "I *am* a Leo."

All of the planets in our solar system have an influence on your personality. Each planet contributes a portion of your overall personality to you. The Sun is traditionally where we start looking at these things, and not just because it's the easiest body in the Solar System to find (except at night of course). The Sun also represents your "life spark," and just like the Sun's role at the center of the Solar System, everything else about your personality would fly off into deep space without it.

Let's talk about *you*. Specifically, let's talk about your Ego, which is the part of you that most wants to hear things about itself.

Carl Jung (one of the Founding Fathers of modern psychology and a big fan of astrology, which is why astrologers like to quote him when they want to look respectable) put forth the notion that everyone is living out a story, with themselves as the protagonist. If that is the case, it might be easiest to think of your Sun Sign as an actor. Actors tend to get "typecast" -- placed in similar roles over and over again, because that's where they do their best work or are most easily recognizable.

Here are the twelve Sun Signs; described with titles typical of the kind of movies those Suns tend to be cast in the most often. If you have a problem with any of it, please: feel free to contact your Agent.

Aries (March 20-April 20)
FAST, FURIOUS, AND ANNOYED

Some astrologers will tell you that the Zodiac starts with Aries because in the Northern Hemisphere, the first day of spring is also the first day of Aries. The truth is that Aries comes first simply because Aries is too impatient to wait.

If you've ever had to baby-sit a hyperactive child whose parents slipped the little darling some sugar before they left for the evening, you're familiar with how Aries energy works. Aries loves a challenge, and if they can't find one, they can usually be counted on to create one. The symbol for Aries is The Ram, long noted for its determination, strength, and fondness for head-butting.

Aries enjoys starting things up: relationships, projects, and chain saws are all favorites. It often doesn't have the same energy for following through on things. This quality can make an Aries highly entertaining to watch and highly frustrating if you're their friend, co-worker, or the neighbour's tree hanging over Aries' driveway. The best advice you can usually give an Aries is to calm down, take it easy, and think things through. This often provokes their temper. Aries isn't necessarily a dangerously temperamental sign, but an Aries is usually at least mildly annoyed about something or other, on some level, at any given point.

The best thing you can do for an Aries is to help them to learn patience. The dumbest thing in the world you can do is expect them to learn it any time soon. That sort of thing usually comes to them later in life, when they are either too tired to be bothered or too busy yelling at kids to get off their lawn.

Aries people usually do things with enthusiasm, which is a good thing if they've stopped to think about what they're doing first. They are straightforward and forthright. The men often embody all the positive traits associated with "manliness," and the women understand that "feminine" and "passive" are two completely different things.

An Aries will often put a great deal of time and energy into their relationships, not necessarily because they are "relationship-oriented." They have a natural tendency to "not get it" with the opposite sex a little more than the other signs. But, given their fiercely competitive natures, if the relationship isn't going to work out they at least want to be on the "winning side" of the break-up. If getting divorced were an Olympic sport, Aries would always be going for the gold.

Taurus (April 20-May 20)
IT'S ALL TOO MUCH II: THE POSSESSING

Have you ever been half starved and had to wait in line at a fast food place while three people in front of you slowly deliberate over their very large orders? That line in front of you was Taurus.

Taurus isn't really greedy, gluttonous, covetous or jealous. It's just that they truly love money, material possessions, eating, and keeping all their stuff. Taurus is represented by the Bull, which is far and away the slowest and meatiest of the Zodiac symbols. In geometry, a "torus" is a doughnut shape, which is entirely appropriate for Taurus. Tauruses love fried food, especially if someone else paid for it. Although Tauruses are big spenders, they also like to save. This central paradox leads many Tauruses to go broke by purchasing things on sale.

Tauruses are excellent at saving energy, which they do by moving slowly. They have a reputation for being sexy and sensuous, which is generally true -- of course; things usually look more sexy and sensuous when they're filmed in slow motion. Taurus likes to deliberate a lot before they make an important decision, and they like to have a lot of options to deliberate over. If you were re-inventing the Zodiac today, instead of a bull, you wouldn't be too far off making Taurus the Buffet Table.

Taurus people like to own pretty things, and they like to *be* pretty things. Almost any Taurus has too much of something in their lives (by other peoples standards), whether it be purses, Green Lantern action figures, lovers, or belly fat.

Tauruses aren't usually big fans of adventure, unless you count a 9 AM doorbuster shoe sale as "an adventure." They are (overall) a sweet and kind people who have larger than average hearts and larger than average security issues. Treat them kindly and tell them every once in a while they're pretty (yes, even the male Tauruses) and they can be remarkably easy to get along with. That is, unless you happen to be after their lover, material possessions, or doughnuts. At that point you are likely to provoke their temper. Tauruses are usually slow to anger, but once they get started their rage can be almost unstoppable. Think "Pamplona."

Taurus people are generally reliable and steady, and they naturally lend an air of stability to any environment they find themselves in. The men of this sign tend to be reassuringly secure (at least in appearance -- they know to keep the twitchiness on the inside). And generally, Taurus women embody all the qualities that men's mothers told them they should marry.

Gemini (May 21-June 21)
TALKBACK, AND TALKBACK AGAIN

Most scientists believe that life on Earth arose as a result of millions of years of random interactions, accidents, and happenstance. Thus, it appears that God is a Gemini.

The symbol for Gemini is The Twins. That leads many people to think Geminis have split personalities. This is an unfair characterization: most twins are able to agree on things and function together better than a lot of Geminis can. Gemini is the sign most likely to be told that they are over-thinking things. This is because they have a remarkable gift for seeing several sides of an issue at once, even if in fact there aren't any other sides. And often, Gemini is able to resolve and/or encompass contradictions better than most people. The primly dressed woman in the choir at church with the inverted pentagram tattoo on her ankle is probably a Gemini.

Geminis are prone to fidgeting, restlessness, nervousness, and biting their nails... interspersed with periods of quiet thoughtfulness, calm, and biting other people's nails. Telling a Gemini to "settle down" is a little like telling a peacock to stop showing off.

Geminis are often popular -- the life of the party. If all of life were a party, Geminis would likely rule the world. As it stands though, most Geminis are barely able to rule themselves, let alone anyone else. They make for gifted speakers, interesting teachers, and notorious swingers. They can be highly diplomatic when they put their minds to it, largely because they've had a lot of practice at thinking about which excuse for their behavior to present first.

The Twins aren't usually very materialistic. They learned long ago that most material possessions aren't that interesting, or will break if you play with them too much in an attempt to make them interesting. This relative lack of impulse control makes them popular with bartenders and credit card companies.

Geminis are usually charming and intelligent. If there is something they don't know, they know where to find the information... or at least they know enough to fake it until they figure it out. The men are interesting and friendly, and the women are usually the life of the party.

Romantically, Geminis are often good at maintaining relationships. You can usually tell by the number of relationship books they own and the number of studies they can cite all wisdom gained from their numerous relationships. And one day, when the rest of the world actually catches up with the advice in relationship books, you'll see actual visible proof that Geminis are good at maintaining these things. Until then, Gemini will keep returning to various Internet dating sites until they find someone or other as good at maintaining relationships as *they* are. Any Gemini reading this paragraph will probably agree. The rest of you spotted the sarcasm.

Cancer (June 22-July 22)
HOME IS WHERE THE HEART HIDES

Crabs have evolved thick, impenetrable shells as an evolutionary defense against being boiled and served with melted butter. And, like a crab, cancers have evolved their personalities to defend their sweet, tasty insides from invaders. Cancers have developed a reputation for being oversensitive, which is not surprising when the symbol for their sign is a crawly thing that's named after a deadly illness.

When the ancient Romans had an unwanted child, they would often carry it off into the woods and leave it to die. When you tell most people that, they are horrified. When you tell most Cancers that, they will (on one level or another) relate it to a story from their own childhood, real or imagined. Cancers never forget a slight or an insult. Whereas other signs can usually "get over it," Cancers tend to file these things away for future reference.

Cancers are sweet, kind, caring and passionate people who often choose to hide it behind a mask of stiff, snarky indifference. Being as caring as they are is not an easy thing in a world full of jerks, thus they often disguise themselves as even bigger jerks than everyone else. You can usually see that sensitivity of theirs if you look deeply into their big sensitive eyes, but don't be surprised if they smack you one for it. No one is supposed to know these things about them, and by reading this book you've probably been quietly added to their Potential Enemies list.

Crabs are imaginative beings. Most people build castles in the sky at one point or another in their lives, but Cancers frequently try to move in and surround it with a shark-filled moat.

Once you have won over a Cancer to your side, they are likely to be your strongest supporter. They are generally good with money and resources. Cancer men are the type who can both fix the toilet and change a baby, and the women are sweet and caring.

Cancers are kind, loving and supportive when they are in a committed relationship. This is probably because by the time you get one to that point, they are too exhausted from fighting it to make any more trouble. They take a genuine, active interest in their children, in part because Cancer loves nothing better than to have someone new to project their complexes onto.

Leo (July 23-August 22)
CAPTAIN DRAMA AND THE
GLITTER SQUAD

The sign of Leo is ruled by the Sun, and the Sun rules the Ego. Thus, if a person's Sun is in Leo, it's a little like the inmates are running the asylum. Leos are frequently mistaken for being pompous and/or self-important. This is a common mistake: it isn't a celebrity's fault that he gets used to adoration and attention, so it probably isn't his fault that he ends up in rehab six months after his show has been cancelled. After all, egos require a lot of support – which is why Leo can often be found bitching loudly about child support payments. A Leo's idea of hell is a place where no one notices them, except momentarily to comment on Leo's bad hair day.

Lion People are fond of sports and games, whether it's football, romance, or wrestling with the neighbour's dog in the back yard. They tend to be fond of small animals, because small animals don't care when you're being clownish. In fact, small animals often prefer that approach from humans. This is why many Leos have their most successful relationships with pets. Pets accept you for who you truly are, and that sort of thing is incredibly valuable to Leos. A mere human, on the other hand, sometimes doesn't appreciate it when a Leo is overwhelmed by their cuteness and *just has to give you a squeeze right now!*

Leos are fond of romance, and are usually good at it. They love the thrill of the hunt and the sweetness and affection that come with the early stages of a relationship. Follow-thorough into the long term isn't their strong suit however, which is why Leos can often be found defending themselves against paternity suits, often pausing to hit on whoever is behind the counter as they file another delaying motion.

Leos are generous and kind by nature, which often helps others put up with their occasionally child-like antics. They tend to get away with a lot because they're generally pretty sexy. Even the less-than-sexy ones can be pretty entertaining to watch when they're trying to be seductive. Any sign can put a mirror on the bedroom ceiling, but Leo is the one who will make sure the lighting is right.

If you want to make a Leo happy, buy them something shiny. It doesn't have to be big (but it helps), and it doesn't have to be expensive (but should probably look it). Leos are bright, shiny people and are attracted to inanimate objects that share that quality. Left to its own devices, Leo would probably build itself a nest made out of tinfoil.

Leo men and women can both be incredibly supportive. The men are generally well loved by women and respected by men, and Leo women are fierce defenders of their home and children. In a domestic situation, Leos like to be the queen of the castle yes, even the male Leos.

Virgo (August 23-September 22)
ALMOST PERFECT II: THE CRITIQUING

The symbol for Virgo is the Virgin, which is in some ways the most misleading of all the Zodiac symbols. Virgos have just as much of a sex drive as anyone else: they're just less likely to be caught at it. They are patient, organized, and efficient people... although they will complain to you that they aren't organized or efficient enough, even when it's obvious they're better at that sort of thing than you are. Although slovenly and unkempt Virgos do exist, they are rare. Even the slovenly Virgos tend to have some area of their lives well-ordered and running efficiently... usually, their large collection of obsessions and neuroses.

People tend to think of Virgos as a little on the cold or indifferent side. This can make Virgos annoying to others, which can hurt a Virgo's feelings. They usually deal with that by presenting themselves as being a little cold or indifferent.

Virgos tend to be intelligent and focused workers, especially if the job involves organizing, cleaning, or being a martyr. They fall into the martyr role easily, being sensitive and caring people who always want to make things better. Although intelligent and knowledgeable, they often lack that sense of a "big picture." In other words: they tend to know where all the fire exits are but waste too much time cleaning out their desks when the building actually bursts into flames.

They also have a keen interest in health and medical matters. If you find yourself out on a first date and are on the receiving end of a long dissertation about how you should have ordered the white wine instead of the red, because there was just a study that showed a connection between red wine and Irritable Bowel Syndrome, you are probably dating a Virgo.

Virgos are usually intelligent and thoughtful. Virgo men can be as detail-oriented as an accountant yet charming and personable. Virgo women know how to take care of you in bed and can tell you where you left you pants afterwards.

Virgos are good at relationships, provided you've overcome their detailed preconceptions of what a mate should be and you manage to get a second date with one. Most people who break up with a Virgo do so because, on one level or another, they suspect Virgo has carefully filed and indexed them rather than actually *committing* to them.

Libra (September 23-October 22)
ISN'T IT ROMANTIC? WELL, *ISN'T IT*???

The symbol for Libra is The Scales, which is entirely appropriate. Libras love weighing things: whether to buy this shirt or that shirt, what to say to their creditors to keep them quiet for a while, their odds of getting attention at the bar tonight, and themselves (followed by the traditional complaining). They are considered to be a peaceful, agreeable, partnership-oriented person... which is largely a scam. Ultimately, Libras aren't any more accommodating as anyone else: they simply have a gift for subtle persuasion of both themselves and others.

Libras aren't actually any more attractive than anyone else, but they tend to come across that way because they *think* they're attractive. Having unintentionally mastered that particular psychological trick, their next move is to cruise the horizon for a mate, like The Terminator scanning for someone to kill. Libra is often considered to be the "romantic" sign. And if by "romantic" you mean "having your way with someone and making them think it was their idea in the first place," you'd be right. That doesn't mean they are oversexed... once in a relationship, Libra can be as boring as everyone else.

Libras often appear to have little or no problem in life. That's because they have mastered the art of projection: they don't have control issues... *you're* the one who's acting up.

Libras like making things pretty. Deep down, all Libras have an Interior Decorator lurking within them. Telling someone how to dress, what color to paint their living room, and which pillow shams to go with are Libra Heaven, especially if it's someone else footing the bill. Libras aren't greedy or materialistic at all... they just like pretty things, which usually cost a lot. And when it comes to pretty things that cost a lot, they usually have terrible impulse control.

Libras are charming and affectionate people. The men are usually those rare males who actually remember your birthday and your favorite color. Libra women bring a "hostess with the mostest" quality to everything they do.

Being considered "the relationship sign," Libras often act like they have to prove it. This can make their partners frustrated, because in relationships the goal itself is not "how hard you try."

Scorpio (October 23-November 21)
DEATH SQUAD OF ONE

Scorpios are the most likely sign to have a complex about what sign there are. And for good reason: Scorpios have accumulated a reputation for being vengeful, wilful, and oversexed. This is inherently unfair to a Scorpio. They aren't any worse than anyone else... they're just far more focused about it when they *are* being awful.

The symbol for Scorpio is the scorpion, which is a creature capable of surviving and thriving in a wide variety of difficult environments. Biologists point out that this is due to their tough build and a stinger in the tail. The truth, however, is that most scorpions are just too stubborn to die under normal circumstances. And, in the event you have one wanting to kill you, they are unlikely to give up until they've achieved that goal too.

Scorpios are easy to annoy. All you have to do is invade their privacy, ask too many questions, or turn them down for sex. They make excellent reporters and detectives, which are career paths noted for involvement with invading people's privacy, asking too many questions, and sex. This is often balanced out by a great deal of inner strength and wisdom, which was usually hard-won after years of being told they're too intense.

Once a Scorpio sets their mind to something, they are incredibly difficult to stop. And they generally don't take it well if you try. Remember that friend of yours when you were a kid who totally freaked out when he lost a game of Monopoly? That kid was probably a Scorpio.

Scorpios are fierce warriors for a just cause. The men combine the best traits of Casanova and James Bond. Scorpio women know what sexy is, they know when to use it, and they use it well.

Scorpios commit a lot of time and energy to their relationships. When a Scorpio's relationship fails, it's probably because they've forgotten that walking hand-in-hand with someone is difficult to do when you always insist on having the *upper* hand.

Sagittarius (November 22-December 21)
ROAD TRIP II: WHO NEEDS A MAP?

The symbol for Sagittarius is the Centaur. That's because (although anyone can make a horse's ass of themselves) Sagittarians are actually *born* that way. They have an open, trusting, and bouncy approach to life, which is perhaps why they are prone to bouncing into open pits more than any other sign. Their faith
in life is so deeply wired into them that they often literally don't bother to look where they are going, and thus tend to be accident-prone. That's also the excuse they use for most of their relationship failures.

Sagittarians have a reputation for being freedom-loving and independent. This is how they like to see it -- everyone else merely thinks of them as being reckless and not taking direction well.

People are rarely surprised when a gay Sagittarius comes out of the closet, because they were usually broadcasting it to the world without trying. You can usually count on a Sagittarius to broadcast whatever is on their mind... their kid, their complaints about work, the details of their hernia operation, and so on. They are considered to be natural communicators, which is a nice way of saying they have an open-mouth policy. In the classic fairy tale "The Emperor's New Clothes," the kid who pointed out that the Emperor was actually naked was probably a Sagittarius. And if the Emperor had been one too, he would have probably countered with something like "Yeah, and it's GREAT! How do you all like my junk?"

Sagittarius is a natural cheerleader and mood-booster when you need it most. They are often the one friend who is really there for you when you need a friend. That's likely because they understand fairness, and you've already had to bail *their* irresponsible ass out of trouble previously. The men of this sign are usually entertaining and friendly, and the women will pick you up, dust you off, and send you back into the battle with a smile on your face.

Sagittarians love the fun of romance and relationships, which tends to make them fun and romantic partners. Unfortunately they also love to play with things until they break. That, and they didn't really mean to sleep with your cousin   it just sort of happened that way.

Capricorn (December 22-January 19)
COMMAND AND CONTROL,
GROUSE AND COMPLAIN

The symbol for Capricorn is The Goat, but the ancient Babylonian symbol was a weird-looking goat/fish hybrid, because ancient Babylonians didn't have All Terrain Vehicles, which would have described Capricorn pretty well. They are solid and steady in almost every environment, and don't mind running you over to get to where they're going.

They usually worry too much about things, and even the happy ones usually end up sprouting worry lines on their forehead a little sooner than everyone else. They aren't necessarily more prone to depression than any other sign, but they are certainly more at home than most in that state of mind. What usually pulls them though is the solid determination that somehow life will be better if they can arrange things more logically.

Capricorns understand the value of keeping their nose to the grindstone, and Capricorn bosses usually keep their employee's noses ground to the cheekbones.

Goat People are usually the stable base you can build just about anything on. The men are usually reliable and hard-working.

The women are sensitive enough to be hurt about all the right things, but brave enough to not let it show too much.

Capricorns can make a relationship work with ruthless efficiency. This would make them an excellent choice for a mate, provided you enjoy the sound of a romantic relationship based on "ruthless efficiency." They are particularly morose after a break-up, until they resolve to make the next one work out, even if it kills both parties involved.

Aquarius (January 20-February 19)
INVADERS FROM URANUS: RAISING A STINK

The symbol for Aquarius is The Water Bearer, which is confusing because Aquarius isn't a "water sign," it's an "air sign". And when you combine atmosphere and moisture, you get fog. That pretty much describes what the thought processes of a typical Aquarius looks like to an outside observer. Aquarius is the sign most likely to have learned that "I gotta be me" is *not* a valid legal defence.

Aquarians have a reputation for being forward-thinking and rebellious. That's because they'd rather organize a sit-in than follow directions at work. Whereas most people will look at the crack in a dam and fear disaster, a typical Aquarius will simply stick his finger in -- although whether they're doing it to stop the leak or pry it open wider is anyone's guess. They tend to be comfortable with the scientific, analytical mindset, which tends to make them excellent researchers and awkward first dates: no one wants to be dissected over wine and pasta.

Aquarius people have both a strong independent streak and an appreciation for the thoughts and company of others. This makes them both excellent leaders who understand the strengths of the "herd mentality" but also the one most likely to run off on their own and get themselves eaten by a wolf.

Often, Aquarians have a fondness for fantasy, science fiction, and romantic historical fiction. That's because "the here and now" is a really awkward place to spend all your time especially if you're a chronic misfit like Aquarius. They can be excellent lovers, but you may always have the sneaking suspicion that they have just as much affection for their sex toys as they do for you.

Aquarians are intelligent, creative and accepting. The men can be equally presentable and at home either in public or private, and the women have a zappy appeal that makes them natural attention-magnets.

In a relationship, Aquarius has a tendency to put the other person and the relationship itself on a pedestal of idealism. That makes them the ideal mate, provided they manage to partner with an ideal rather than a human being. Otherwise, the perfect Aquarian relationship will have to wait for further advances in robotics.

Pisces (February 19-March 20)
LIVING THE DREAM, WAKING UP WITH A STRANGER

Have you ever had that experience where you are drunk enough to do something that you know is probably a bad idea, yet still been sober enough to realize it while you're doing it? Congratulations... you have had The Pisces Experience.

The symbol for Pisces is The Fish. Or rather, two fishes, headed in opposite directions, and neither one aware of the fact that they are completely surrounded by water. Pisces people tend to be focus on the spiritual and the higher values in life. This is a nice way of saying that they aren't the most practical creatures on the planet.

Pisces is naturally in tune with spiritual concepts like karma. They are the kind of people who can empathize with a dog about its mishandling as a puppy while that dog is biting them. This quality tends to make them natural "jerk magnets." On the upside, they are wonderfully compassionate lovers and companions: just ask any jerk.

Fish folks love fantasy and adventure tales, and they have a peculiar gift for turning their lives into fantasy adventure tales. Unfortunately for Pisces, there is a shortage of magic wands and Lost Arks lying around to

41

bring these stories to a successful resolution. Thus Pisces will often invest a lot of their time and energy into alcohol and/or drugs, which usually provide a much more predictable resolution than "real life" ever could.

Pisces are at heart sweet, kind, caring people. The men have that "sensitive male" quality women love, and the women have a natural femininity that drives men wild. A

Pisces' relationships usually fall into one of two categories: those that start out in an idealistic haze but end up in a wreck, and those that started as wrecks but are covered up with a thick layer of idealistic haze. All relationships start with a hormonal high, which is natural territory for a Pisces. It's just a shame they're so damned bad at sobering up.

Part Two: The Moon
Tell Me Where It Hurts

As important as your Sun Sign is, your Moon is equally important. The Sun is the outfit you wear to work every day, but The Moon is what you slip into at home to be comfortable.

The Sun and Moon make for a classic odd couple: one is bright and shiny; the other one is soft and changeable. Both are equally important when it comes to who you truly are, but often the Sun's inherent showiness obscures the Moon side of your persona. That's just fine by the Moon: it's inherently sensitive, and often prefers that you pay more attention to something else. When people complain that others don't know "the real me," they are probably referring to their Moon.

Your Moon is how you react to your world on an instinctual level, before things like language and social roles get in the way. When a baby cries because he's hungry or tired or uncomfortable or bored, it's his Moon Sign talking. Likewise, when the people closest to you yell at you because they are hungry or tired or uncomfortable or bored (or you aren't playing your role in what they think the relationship should be) you've probably provoked their Moon somehow.

The Moon is also the place where you are most likely to store any and all of your childhood emotional issues. The following descriptions are accompanied by re-tellings of popular children's stories, Moon-sign style. Get your milk and cookies, and enjoy.

Moon in Aries

You enjoy being supportive of the people you care about, and tend to think of yourself as kind of a cheerleader for them. Unfortunately, others often tend to think of you more as a drill sergeant. Your emotional nature is impulsive and dashing, and your impulses often leave you dashing around and running a few people over. You have a lot of love to give, and you're going to give it *right now*. Moon in Aries is reasonably vulnerable to emotional bruising, and you probably consider this to be your greatest weakness. The best defence is a strong offence, and you often risk being strongly offensive.

Moon in Aries responds well to competitive games and sports, like boxing, football, or spouse-stealing. This placement can get depressed, but responds well to physical activity like aerobics or chasing after impossible relationships. People with this placement take fierce pride in their children and families, and can always be counted on to join in a brawl with the other parents at a Little League game. Sometimes they invest so much of their identity in their children that the kids end up being the ones who goes off to work to pay the bills while the parent stays at home and cries for candy. Despite all this, they are warm and loving people.

"...And what great big teeth you have!"
Red Riding Hood said to the figure under the blankets.

"All the better to EAT you with!" The Big Bad Wolf said as he sprang from the bed. Red Riding Hood quickly crammed her picnic basket into the Wolf's mouth.

"Listen pal," she said, "I came here for extra credit on my Senior Home Care courses. I don't care who you are or what you think you're doing, but you're gonna sit down, shut up, and start knitting me a sweater."

Red then sat next to the bed and produced a clip board. "This is my student evaluation form. I'll fill it out for you. Sign here..."

Moon in Taurus

The sign of the Bull is where the Moon is "exalted." In other words, it is considered to be at its strongest and do its best work. And you are excellent at doing a lot of Moon-related things: being nurturing and supportive, making people feel comfortable with you, and binge eating. You are the kind of person who naturally puts others at ease, like a good hostage negotiator. Moon in Taurus people tend to be slow to anger, but once they get to that point, a hostage negotiator is often required. This is especially true if the cause of the wrath is hunger. Moon in Taurus people love to chow down. You have a fondness for lazing around and eating that can only be matched by an overweight, neutered cat.

Moon in Taurus strives to find strength and stability in its relationships and children, and since those are rare qualities, Moon in Taurus is often quietly disappointed with the people closest to it. Material security is important to you, and you can often be found talking loudly about your investments, whether financial or emotional. And those investments frequently tend to under perform compared to your long-term projections. You make an excellent shoulder to cry on, are physically affectionate, and can probably cook a mean pot roast.

Beauty's sleep was interrupted by frantic hacking and slashing sounds coming from outside. The handsome Prince was fighting his way through the wall of thorns that had magically sprung up around the castle. "I suppose I should get up and help him," Beauty said to herself.

Then she paused to contemplate the softness of the bed she laid on, and the warmth of the thick eider down duvet that covered her. "Then again," she said to herself as she rolled over and prepared to go back to sleep, "there's nothing wrong with a girl making a man work for it a little. I hope he brought Chinese food..."

Moon in Gemini

People with Moon in Gemini have just as many feelings as anyone else, but tend to prefer intellectualizing them in an attempt to make them go away. Thus, the people they care about them the most have an unfortunate tendency to go away. You often try to think your way around emotional issues, which is usually about as effective as you'd think it is. In many ways, you are more comfortable with a little of everything rather than a lot of something specific. Rather than trying to find someone to hook up with at the party and go home, you're most likely comfortable staying until it shuts down, carrying the hors d'oevres tray around to everyone left behind.

You can more than hold up your end in a debate, and often welcome the opportunity to defend your position. That's because you have learned that "defending your position" is not the same as "discussing your feelings," and is generally a lot safer. Also, you tend to be better at words than actions. Nonetheless, you are a sprightly companion, are well-liked by others, and when you put your mind to it you can talk your way out of almost any sticky situation. People with Moon in Gemini often get bored quickly with their playthings... but play well with them before they reach that point.

"And there she is NOW!" Baby Bear shouted as he pointed at Goldilocks hiding in the corner.

"Hey guys, glad you could make it!" Goldilocks said as she smiled wide and opened her arms in greeting. "I thought you should know I got rid of that porridge for you. I think it was a little off. Mama Bear... you look fantastic! Have you lost weight recently? And Papa Bear... hey, how you doing? I haven't seen you since that time at the bar when you were with Mrs. Kodiak!"

"What were you doing with that Kodiak slut?" Mama Bear shouted angrily at Papa Bear. A fierce argument broke out between the two of them, and Baby Bear ran to his room and cried.

By the time the dust had settled, Goldilocks was long gone.

Moon in Cancer

No one gets through childhood without developing a few issues, but people with Moon in Cancer often seem to have more than most. At the same time, they often put more effort into hiding them than the average person. These two qualities can make you a look a little neurotic, which is actually a good thing... because deep down you're probably pretty neurotic. You are highly creative and deeply imaginative, and this can make you imagine personal slights and insults where none was intended. You cry at sad movies and get angry when anyone catches you at it. Moon in Cancer is sensitive to its emotional environment, and spends a lot of time and energy defending against it.

When you do let your guard down and truly let someone into your heart, you cling to them like a barnacle. This doesn't mean they are immune to your mood swings: you just have to hope they are as understanding and accepting of them as you are. Moon in Cancer is naturally protective of the weak and the underdog. You would make an excellent defender of social justice, except that you're afraid someone might see you at it and laugh. You have long and durable memory for the wrongs and insults committed against you. Even the biggest

Macho Man with Moon in Cancer has a deeply ingrained maternal side.

Under a big tree in the woods, there sits a tuffet of grass, unoccupied except for an untouched bowl of curds and whey. Every ten minutes or so an antenna extends from behind the tree, and the silence is broken by the beeping of the SpiderScan 4000 Arachnid detector. After an hour or so of this, Miss Muffett emerges from behind the tree and slowly and carefully approaches the bowl. She finally sits down and begins to eat it.

A few minutes later a gentle breeze brings a butterfly flitting into Miss Muffett's view. Muffett pulls a sawed-off shotgun out from under her skirt and with a single skilful shot blows the butterfly away.

"Well... they're ALMOST like a spider," she says.

Moon in Leo

You are warm and loving and playful, like a big pussycat. Actually, like a lion. They call a group of lions a "pride," and pride can be a central issue with you. You expect your warm and loving nature to be reflected back at you more than most do, and when those around you fall short (by your standards) you can become a ruthless predator. It was probably someone with Moon in Leo who invented those "My Child is an Honor Student" bumper stickers. You have high standards for yourself, and like to play fair, and you usually manage to live by those standards yourself. And when you fall short of those standards yourself, you feel bad... but can justify it to others loudly all day long.

You are fond of jewellery and luxury. Moon in Leo people enjoy loud dramatic relationships, loud dramatic break-ups, and loud dramatic cars. All this amplified emotion can be exactly what someone else is looking for in a partner, but it can just as easily drive people away. Fortunately, your better qualities usually win out, and you can be magnanimous and forgiving. When things are going well and you are in a good mood, romance with you can be as memorable as the restraining order that leads to the break-up.

Belle squealed with delight as she hugged the handsome prince, recently restored to life and transformed back from his beastly form. "Oh, I love you so! And we'll have the most wonderful wedding. There will be a horse-drawn carriage and a symphony and a three day feast and we'll have the moat re-lined and my wedding dress will be encrusted in diamonds and all my cousins and friends from college will be there and there'll be magicians and jugglers and clowns and --"

The handsome prince broke free from Belle's embrace. He walked towards the door, stopping only to fish in his pocket and toss a key to Belle. "Here. You might as well take it all now" he said as he walked to the door. "I'm going to go live in the woods. Call me some time."

"But you don't have a cell phone!" she shouted after him as the door slammed shut.

Moon in Virgo

Like the traditional sign of The Virgin it is associated with, Moon in Virgo has a reputation for being cautious and modest. These qualities make it easy for others to mistakenly believe you are a cold fish, or a calculating bitch. And -- usually -- that is a mistake. Your mind has a fairly firm grip on how you express your feelings. Rather than gush over the ones you love, you prefer to express your innermost feelings through dietary tips, sanitary wipes, and gentle nagging. In part, this is because you are overly worried about exposing your sensitivity to others. Others have to leap a lot of hurdles to get to know you really well, but the effort is usually worth it.

You tend to intellectualize your feelings and to compile mental lists of reason why you shouldn't do or feel this or that. If having the appearance of self-control were a handicap, you would automatically get your own parking space everywhere you go. People with Moon in Virgo generally don't think their homes are clean or orderly enough, even though your underwear is probably filed and indexed by age, color, and material. When you put your mind to it, you can be terribly cunning and calculating with your emotions. Fortunately you usually use this for good rather than ill. Usually.

"So you see," Goldilocks said as she finished writing the formula out on the white board, "mixing the contents of bowls A, B, and C causes a thermal equilibrium in which all three bowls of porridge come out just right."

Mama Bear yawned. "Can we kill her yet?" she whispered to Papa Bear.

Goldilocks continued. "Also, while you were out, I had time to review your utility bills and found some interesting patterns in your energy usage. If you will now all please refer to the graph on page twelve of the reports I've given you..."

Moon in Libra

Moon in Libra is sweet and kind and caring... or possibly a total pushover who can't stand for themselves. The two are often mistaken for each other, but especially in people with this Moon placement. People tend not to have too many bad things to say about you, but sometimes that's because you haven't made that much of an impression one way or another. You'd think that your finer qualities would make you more appreciated by others, and that is often the case. Unfortunately, in a dog-eat-dog world, you are often appreciated in the same way a dog appreciates a slice of bacon.

You have a natural empathy with others, and this can make you indecisive. And you are likely to be accommodating enough to let others make a lot of decisions for you, whether you're conscious of it or not. You would make a gifted speaker or activist for human rights and equality issues, if you can get over your natural urge to not rock the boat. When Moon in Libra develops control issues, it usually does so because "it's for your own good." Moon in Libra is often "in love with love," which is much easier and safer than actually being in love with an actual *person*.

The Prince kneeled down beside the still form of the Princess and placed a single gentle kiss upon her lips. Her eyes fluttered and she awoke. "Oh, that was lovely," she said. "Do it again."

The Prince kissed her again. After a moment she reached up to straighten his collar. "It must have been a lot of work getting in here. Your shirt is wrinkled. And are you sure this is a good color for you? Green would have worked better with your eyes. "Do you like what I've done with our room? I got the drapes on sale."

" 'Our' room?" The Prince asked. "What do you mean?"

"Well, of course, silly boy, we have to get married now. I want six children. You can name the odd-numbered ones if you like. And we can have the ceremony on either a Thursday or a Saturday, your choice. And of course you'll have approval over the guest list, and the dinner.... except I really want Beef Wellington."

"I'm sorry," The Prince said. "What was your name again...?"

Moon in Scorpio

Moon in Scorpio has a difficult reputation among a lot of astrologers. People with this placement are often accused of being jealous, controlling, spiteful, and hard to get along with when they are annoyed. That's unfortunate, because it isn't your fault that people are so unfaithful, stupid, and disagreeable. It's just lucky for everyone else that you are here to set them straight, loudly and repeatedly, until they either get the point or stop breathing.

People with Moon in Scorpio have deep, intense feelings. If there is anything "surface" about you at all, it's only for the same reason that the trap-door spider hunts the way it does: it's more efficient to let your prey come to you and then be surprised. On the positive side, people rarely have to guess how you feel about them. You can be fiercely loyal and unswerving in your opinions. You can also be unswerving to avoid a collision with someone who is aiming for the same parking spot you had your eye on.

"M-m-my, wh-what b-big eyes y-you have," The Big Bad Wolf stuttered nervously as the red pinpoint of the laser sight danced on his chest.

"That's right... "Granny," Little Red Riding Hood said. "And what are you going to do with them?"

"I -- I'm going to... see you with them?" The Wolf hazarded.

"No!" Little Red shouted as she slapped the Wolf across the face. "you're going to use them to find the kitchen. There, you will cough up Grandma, and the two of you are going to bake me cookies. Lots of cookies. And you're going to do it until you get it right!"

The Wolf sobbed. "Isn't some Woodsman supposed to come in at this point and end my suffering?" The Wolf whimpered.

"Change of plans, Wolfie," Red said. "He pissed me off on the way over here. He won't be going ANYWHERE for a while..."

Moon in Sagittarius

You are probably what people consider to be "the life of the party." Unfortunately for you, you also bring that vibe to court hearings and funerals where perhaps that vibe doesn't belong. People with Moon in Sagittarius are often described as "irrepressible," and for good reason: there are many times when you can or should be repressed. You are caring and sympathetic and have a hard time seeing other people down or depressed. This makes you a supportive friend and makes you tend to take it far too easy on people who should be considered your enemy. Moon in Sagittarius can become depressed, and on those rare occasions when it does, it throws everything into it.

Moon in Sagittarius often enjoys a wide circle of friends and often takes a playful, fun approach to its closest relationships. This can be a problem when your partner gets tired of you always being out playing with your friends. You mean well, of course, but have a hard time understanding that no, we *can't* always "just get along." Moon in Sagittarius functions best in an environment of like-minded individuals, which (in your case) often means children and dogs. You often have a gift for seeing the future, which is a good thing, because you don't pay enough attention to the here and now.

"Little pig, little pig, let me in!" The Wolf shouted at the Brick House. After a moment, a silver projectile launched from the upstairs window and landed at the Wolf's feet. It was a beer can.

"Okay, drink that first!" a voice said from inside.

The Wolf did so, and began to shout again at the House. "Little pig, little pig --"

Another can flew out the window. "Not yet. Keep drinking!" the little voice said from inside the house, where loud dance music soon began thumping.

This process repeated itself for another hour and a half. By the end of the evening, The Big Bad Wolf was inside the brick house, lying on the floor and moaning "I love you guys!" to his new-found friends. He spent most of the night alternately singing and complaining about his lacklustre love life to the Three Little Pigs.

The next morning, The Big Bad Wolf awoke before the pigs did, and he promptly ate them.

Moon in Capricorn

Just as Moon in Sagittarius is the life of the party, Moon in Capricorn is the clean-up crew that necessarily must follow afterwards. You have a reputation for being calm, contained, and maybe a little distant. This is because you have a tremendous depth of feeling that needs to be protected by maintaining emotional self-control. This can either eventually drive yourself or those who care about you completely nuts. Moon in Capricorn often comes across as managing its personal relationships with ruthless efficiency, which may be wise but isn't terribly romantic.

You usually find one thing, place, or person in which to place your sense of emotional security. If that's another person, you are probably fairly young (and haven't learned how untrustworthy humans can be) or fairly old (and have spent most of your life overcoming your suspicions). Your defensiveness can be strangely appealing to other people who enjoy solving emotional mysteries, and can be frustrating as hell to everyone else. Moon in Capricorn strives for emotional self-sufficiency, which is as admirable as it is impossible.

"Tell me my name and you can have your baby!" The little man said.

"It's Rumpelstiltskin!" the Miller's Daughter said triumphantly.

Rumpelstiltskin pondered this for a moment, and then removed a contract from his back pocket. "Here you go," he said as he handed it to her. "Spell it right, otherwise the agreement is void!"

The Miller's Daughter thought about this for a moment and then filled in the form. Rumpelstiltskin examined it and found that, surprisingly, she had gotten it right.

"Okay then," he said. "Now all you have to do is find a Notary before midnight to make it legal and binding."

"But it's 11:30 at night! And it's a Saturday!" The Miller's Daughter shouted in disbelief.

Rumpelstiltskin chuckled. "You shoulda read the fine print on the original agreement, sucker."

Moon in Aquarius

People with Moon in Aquarius have a wonderfully open and accepting approach to life, which makes you a great companion and a terrible security guard. You don't handle jealously well, because others can't tell you who or what you should be... especially given that you may not know those things yourself.

Moon in Aquarius has a wonderful ability to empathize with everyone, to the point where you become both the psychotherapist *and* the guy in the tinfoil hat. You often deal with this by trying to take a step back and logical evaluating your relationships, which may be wise but isn't terribly romantic. You often stop and ask yourself how you feel about things, and often an answer is ages in coming.

Moon in Aquarius recognizes that all men are brothers, and you are always willing to help your brother out -- unless we're talking about an emergency loan, in which case all men are complete strangers and should go away. Nonetheless, people can (and do) find ways to take advantage of you at times. You are rarely cruel or mean, and can't usually stand the thought of hurting anyone. This makes you a wonderful friend and a terrible surgeon.

"*Off with her head!*" The Queen commanded as she pointed at Alice. The Queen's footmen all swarmed on Alice, and she threw up her arms defensively.

Then Alice grabbed several of the footmen and began arranging them in groups of four. "That's not how it's played at all" she said to the Queen. Alice then turned to the footmen in the back of the crowd. "Okay, you guys lie down in a pile, face down. Neatly, now."

"*Off with her head!*" The Queen shouted, more angrily than before.

"Now that's no way to run a poker tournament, Your Majesty." Alice responded. "Here's how it's done." She pointed to the group of four footmen closest to her. "See, I have a pair of eights here. So, Three and Nine, you go stand over there. Now, the two guys at the top of the pile over there? You guys come here." Puzzled, the two footmen at the top of the pile complied. Alice smiled. "Oh boy! Three of a kind!"

"*OFF WITH HER HEAD!!!*"

Moon in Pisces

What a sweet, kind, wonderful, empathic creature you are! You are welcome in any environment and there is always room for you at a gathering, rather like Jell-O at a buffet. And usually, you end up suffering the same fate as Jell-O at a buffet: either ignored because everyone filled up on something more exciting, or swallowed whole and forgotten five minutes after the bill is paid. Being a gentle creature at heart, you are unlikely to stand up for yourself in either eventuality. You are kind to a fault to everyone except perhaps yourself, which is who you usually end up blaming things on.

You have a dreamy vibe to you, and have probably experienced some form of psychic phenomena. This is a good thing, because your analytical skills probably aren't the greatest and you need all the help you can get. Rudeness and unkindness are foreign to you, despite the fact that you are often on the receiving end of it. In a world populated entirely by people with Moon in Pisces, there would be no war or intolerance -- but plenty of sedatives and antidepressants. In your relationships, you have probably given a lot more love than you've received, but are too nice to complain about it.

"Oh, this is terrible, terrible!" Goldilocks sobbed as she laid her head down on the table and pounded her fists, making the dishes jump. "I was lost in the woods, and it wasn't my fault, and I was so hungry... and your porridge looked so good! And I was going to leave a note apologizing! And I was going to leave money and a coupon for more porridge too!"

"And now..." she paused to blow her nose... "Now I'm going to get eaten by bears! And I love bears! They're so cute and fuzzy, how could I not? It's so unfair!"

"Listen, lady, I don't know where you think you are," The Mad Hatter said as he poured himself more tea, "but you're obviously at the wrong party. Now shove off. All that crying is making the Dormouse wet."

Part Three: The Personal Planets
Talk, Love, Fight

In the last two sections, we covered the most useful, basic information as to how people operate within the confines of their own heads and hearts. With that information alone, you can go a long way towards understanding yourself, those you are close to and those you *want to be* close to.

That would be great if that's all there was to it. But life isn't just a matter of "being yourself" (all hippie New Age personal advice aside). It's also a matter of how you interact with others, unless of course you are a complete hermit. And if you're a complete hermit, you either shouldn't bother reading a book with "Love and Seduction" in the title or you desperately need to read it all *right now*.

As we move on from The Sun and Moon, we discover Mercury, which is the planet that rules how your brain works and how you talk to people. Once that conversation has started, Venus comes into play. Venus rules how you express your love, and the kinds of things and activities you love. Then there's Mars. Mars was traditionally the God of War, and yes Mars has a lot to do with your temper. But more importantly, it rules what drives you including your sex drive.

Once you are able to put all these elements together, you'll have a much more complete picture of yourself and others than any simple Sun Sign guide could give you. And you'll be well on your way to not just understanding how astrology really works and (more importantly) how *people* work. Read on, my friend the Great Game of Humanity continues, and you are about to learn how to play it better, more skilfully, and more completely.

Mercury - How You Think (When You Bother To)

The planet Mercury in your birth chart has a lot of things to do with what's on your mind, how your thoughts work, and how you translate those thoughts into words and behaviors. It's the part of you that plays along with game shows at home. These are personal qualities that, to be honest, most people don't get terribly excited about. When people want to learn astrology, it's usually because they want to know why their love life is so screwed up, or why their job is so lousy. But more often than not, those situations exist (or continue to exist) at least in part because of your ability (or lack of ability) to think things through logically or to express your needs.

Be warned: now that we've dealt with your Ego (the Sun) and put the baby down for a nap (the Moon), you can expect a lot of telemarketing calls to start coming in.

Mercury in Aries Aries has a reputation for being a hothead, and Mercury in Aries plays right along. Your thinking and speech are often impulsive and decisive. You can produce a lot of ideas in rapid-fire succession, but you don't usually do all that well with long-term plans and practicality. You would probably be an excellent debater, specializing in quick comebacks and snappy one-liners. Mercury in Aries is much better suited to a rap battle than to debating an amendment to the Tax Code. This placement is excellent for quick, staccato outbursts of speech, finishing other people's sentences, and chewing out the waiter when the order is wrong. Watch for quick little emphatic head-bobs when someone with Mercury in Aries is making a point or really excited about something.

"So yeah, about our new long distance plan: it's good. Really good. So you are going to sign up now, right? Whaddaya mean you don't use long distance? You're talking to me, and I'm in Mumbai. See? Told you so. And just to prove it, I'll call you again tomorrow. Maybe the next day too. Unless of course you accept our time limited offer now. What's the time limit? It expires five minutes after you run out of patience and break down and give us your long-distance business."

Mercury in Taurus

Mercury in Taurus can sometimes get it wrong, but loses few marks because it remembered to show all its work. This placement is often better at making existing ideas work better rather than coming up with that one breakthrough idea. In fact, Mercury in Taurus is likely the one that will spot the obvious flaws in someone else's "breakthrough idea" first. Your thinking has a tendency to be influenced by price, practicality and appearance. Mercury in Taurus usually has good focus when working on an idea. Once you've put your mind to finding a solution, it's only a matter of time until you do find one. It just may take you a very long time. Often people with Mercury in Taurus have a slight tendency to linger on their vowels slightly longer than the average person, as if they're enjoying the pronunciation process a little more than others do.

"By signing up today, you'll save 25% off of the newsstand price. Yes, I understand you don't actually have a dog, but by subscribing to Shih-Tzu Illustrated you'll have all the information at hand to make the right choice should you change your mind about that. Also, the paper is glossy and the little

doggies are 30% more adorable than before... they all have little sweaters on now! Isn't that adorable? Sorry? But... if you're allergic, why are you on my call list for today? We were supposed to call the allergic people yesterday! You must be mistaken."

Mercury in Gemini

Mercury in Gemini is considered to be an excellent placement; these are the people who often get tagged as "bright" early on in school. They also often get labelled "hyperactive" or fidgety; these people are prone to being unable to concentrate in an over-stimulating environment. This placement usually has a talent for trivia games and "thinking outside of the box." You probably know at least a little bit about a lot of different things... and often, that's all it takes to figure out the rest. When someone with Mercury in Gemini is speaking about a matter that excites them, you have to listen twice as carefully for the breaks so you can get your comment in, because they tend to be particularly short and far in between.

"You wouldn't believe how useful our product is! You'll wonder how you ever managed without it. It slices, it dices, and it can cut through a tin can and stays sharp enough to slice a tomato paper-thin! Let your child run around the house with it and it becomes an educational toy! Eliminate household pests! Remove stubborn stains! And that's just the monthly bill... the magazine itself is pretty useful too."

Mercury in Cancer

A Crabby Mercury is an interesting placement: at home with logic, yet deeply attuned to your emotional environment. You'd probably make an excellent marriage counsellor for almost any situation... except probably your own. You're probably bad at lying, except for the lies you've come to believe, which is a phenomenon that can happen to anyone, but maybe to you a little more than others. You likely learn things best by soaking in them and absorbing it all more or less at once. Being aware of the feelings of others around you can help you see through their foibles, or (if you aren't careful) you could end up joining the pitchfork-wielding mob without quite knowing what you're rebelling against. When you want to, your voice probably has an exceptionally comforting tone.

"I understand you don't feel you need a home security system. But have you thought about the safety of your children? You don't have any? Okay, what about your valuables? You don't have -- okay: how would you feel about a complete stranger breaking in and going through your underwear? Ha! Didn't think you'd like that. So, please buy this from

me: my supervisor has been a jerk about my sales all day."

Mercury in Leo

This is considered by some to be a "debilitated" placement, in that you are likely better at hitting the emotional marks than perfectly memorizing your lines. If your director encourages his actors to ad-lib, that's great. If you're negotiating with a banker over the logical reasons why you should be approved for the loan, you'd better bring backup. Strong-willed and focused, you are good at using whatever is at hand to support your logic, whereas others tend to base their logic on the observable data. Whether you know what you're talking about or not, you can sound like an Authority while talking about it. You are likely prone to grand gestures, both in terms of your choice in words and the gestures that accompany them.

"Wow! Incredible! You know, I've been working here for two months and still can't get over how fantastic this thing is! It's the best-selling, shiniest, most famous garden tool ever! It makes weeding so easy you'll swear it's doing all the work! Wait... what do you mean, 'you live in an apartment'? You could still hang your coat on it, and I'll bet none of the neighbors have one! Come on... I'm not going away until you buy one. Maybe two."

Mercury in Virgo

Mercury in Virgo is a strong placement. When you put your mind to it, no one does detail work better than you. There's likely a little alarm bell that goes off inside of you if you or (more likely) anyone else mangles a quote or mispronounces or misuses a word. You have the ability to logically support any of your stances, whether they were born of logic or not. People with Mercury in Virgo have a capacity to learn almost anything, provided they have enough highlighters, sharpened pencils, and a properly organized binder. You likely have a precise, measured tone to your speaking voice, and have a gift for spotting the logical flaws in your opponent's case during a debate.

"So: on your current plan you're paying an average 4.7 cents per minute on your long distance calls. On ours, you'd be paying an average of 4.9 cents per minute, but our rate to Kiribati can't be beat. Yes, I know you don't call Kiribati. But you might. They have some interesting plants there that are being used to find new asthma treatments, and you're sounding a little wheezy. Do you really want to be left out when the inevitable happens and

you're lying there, gasping for breath at your current service provider's bill?"

Mercury in Libra

More often than not, Mercury in Libra tends to see things in terms of the relationships between things and/or people. This makes it an excellent placement for planning the seating arrangement at a party or sorting out who's telling the truth and who's lying, but doesn't function as well at things like doing your taxes. Mercury in Libra is much better suited to tasks like people watching rather than watch repair. Nonetheless, this isn't a "fluffy" placement: when you set your mind to it, you can be thorough and efficient in your intellectual processes. You know how to swear as well as the next guy, but have a better sense for when it will make the most impact, as opposed to doing it every third word.

"...And it comes in a black simulated leather carrying case. That means you'll have all the ability to accessorize with it that you would with actual black leather, but more animal-friendly. Yes, I understand you don't actually need a new hedge clipper, but you'd look great with it. Where should I send this to? What? No, of course you're going to buy one. It was all YOUR idea. Honest! Remember? You don't? Oh well. You don't want me to cry now, do you? Good. How many would you like?"

Mercury in Scorpio

You're probably tired of being told your words and thought processes are "intense" and "serious." The truth is that you do "intense" and "serious" very well. Even if you're just playing a board game with the kids, you are capable of winning with ruthless intensity... and cataloguing your errors if you lose in order to gain vengeance -- um, I mean play better -- next time. You have a talent for finding the hidden weaknesses and back entrance to any fortress you face, and may be more comfortable with that approach, even if the front door is wide open. Mercury in Scorpio has a talent for cutting to the chase, digging in the dirt, and analyzing the effectiveness of potential pick-up lines before selecting one. When you make an effort with your tone of voice, no one does "gravitas" like you can.

"Here's how this is going to play out: I'm going to ask you a few questions about your past vacations. Then I'm going to look at my cheat sheet here and tell you how many hundreds of dollars you would have saved with us. Then you'll object, I'll counter with an improved offer, and then you'll accept. Two months from now, you'll be in your dream

time-share on the beach in Haiti. Everyone's happy. Now, go get your chequebook."

Mercury in Sagittarius

Mercury in Sagittarius hasn't got the reputation for being the most thorough or analytical of placements, but fortunately for you, you've discovered that often The Universe will fill in the details for you as you go along. This Mercury placement is good at absorbing a few general principles, at which time you can probably "fake it 'til you make it" the rest of the way. When facing a major decision, Mercury in Sagittarius can benefit nicely from going for a long walk or a drive, and yet be completely unable to locate the keys or remember what the route back home is. You probably have a better-than-average ability with languages and/or mimicry.

"...And then the three-legged armadillo said, 'I may be slow, but I'm always hard!' Hahaha! Yeah, I love that one. I first heard it in college when I was taking English Lit. Ask me how well THAT paid off for me! Haha. I gotta tell you though... there were a LOT of hotties in those classes. That's why I took 'em, really. That, and to shut my parents up. Oh, anyway, back to what we were discussing before: Funerals are expensive these days. Do you have the coverage you need?"

Mercury in Capricorn

Calling Mercury in Capricorn ruthless, efficient, and single-minded is terribly unfair: you would prefer "goal-oriented and capable." You have a managerial mind that would be excellent running a small office, debugging a complex software issue, or plotting revenge. You benefit from formal education, but probably need more hands-on experience. Properly focused, you can be a Human Lie Detector. You are slightly harder to scam than most others. You can assemble a monthly budget better than anyone, even if you don't necessarily stick to it all that well. Watch for people with Mercury in Capricorn to slightly purse their lips for a fraction of a second before making a spending decision.

"You know, your current long distance provider is costing you more than you realize. First of all, they outsource more of their services than we do, so if you had ALL your services with us, you'd be saving jobs in your own country. Also, have you considered the long-terms costs of not buying one of our plans from me today? I am with your phone company after all, and I'd hate to see anything go wrong with your service. Now, what will you be buying from us today?"

Mercury in Aquarius

The thought processes of people with Mercury in Aquarius are often described as "revolutionary" and "ahead of its time." That's when your ideas work out of course... the rest of the time your ideas are more likely to be described as "a little weird." You have a particular gift for picking up on the right threads to keep a conversation at a crowded party going. Mercury in Aquarius is considered "exalted," which gives you the ability to see that everything happens for a reason, that all things are connected, and if you just tighten that dangly bit over there everything will work much better. You probably remember catchy sayings better than most.

"It's not just a magazine, it's a statement. It says 'I am strong and confident.' It says 'I am informed about my world.' And it also says 'I am up to date on today's greatest entertainment news.' Also, if you order "Clog Dancing Monthly" you'll not only be helping me out, but you'll also be supporting the recycling industry when you throw it out every month right after it arrives. So: are you ready to help me save the planet? Will that be one year's worth, or two?"

Mercury in Pisces

Your imagination isn't entirely impractical, and your practicality is usually pretty imaginative. This isn't usually considered a great placement for Mercury, but you make up for being soft on logic with compassion and a well-developed intuition. In conversations and gatherings, your words and conversation often take on the tone of others, like something in the fridge that starts to smell like whatever it's next to. Mercury in Pisces is sensitive to the human factors involved, and this can sometimes help you find solutions that logic alone couldn't uncover. When you are surrounded by foreigners, you are likely to pick up their accent quickly without even trying.

"In an uncertain world, home security has never been more important. Our company provides the latest in burglar alarm technology, and -- I'm sorry? You aren't interested? But what about all the maniacs out there? You can't afford it? I interrupted your dinner? Oh God, I'm so, so sorry. I feel terrible. I... I feel like I've violated the sanctity of your home and your personal life. What a terrible thing! It must feel like you've been... robbed. Now, let me choke back the tears and tell you about our payment plans..."

Venus - Love, Money, and Candy

Everybody loves Venus. In your birth chart she rules your love style, the things you like to do when you feel lazy, and your fondness for sweets, among other things. These are all things we spend a lot of our time striving for, and these things are also the source of a lot of our heartbreak, waste, and heart disease. There's a temptation to call Venus "The Love Planet," but that would be inaccurate -- any love beyond the kind you feel for a really good cookie is a lot more complex than just one planet can cover. Venus in your birth chart also influences your attitude towards money and material resources. It might be more accurate to call Venus the "Sweetness and Light" planet. Those things are certainly related to how people feel about love and money, in much the same way that a flashy car ad is related to future breakdowns, overdue payments, and fender benders.

Having said that, Venus does have a fair bit to do with who you love, how you love, and *what* you love. While we're looking at Venus through the signs, let's also look at the personal ads she put on the Internet during her last orbit, and some of her responses to the ads others placed. And: why *is* a nice girl like her still single anyway?

Venus in Aries

Venus in Aries is no blushing bride or wallflower: she's into adventure. This is considered a "debilitated" placement for Venus, and maybe that's why she isn't so ladylike in this sign. You often need more than the average amount of attention in a relationship, but if you're doing the relationship right, your partner will return the favor. Venus in Aries people are good at (and are fond of) impulsive romantic gestures, surprise gifts, and stalking. Even women with Venus in Aries like to be the Knight in Shining Armor in their relationships in one form or another. If someone can find a way to keep the excitement ongoing in a relationship with you, they've got someone they can keep for life. Probably, anyway until you get bored that is.

"Dear PantherFan66: Thanks for writing back! To answer your question, yes I am still available and still interested. So here's what I propose: Friday, 8 PM, Mickey McFlynn's. Get there 15 minutes early -- I want one of those tables in the back corner. order the nachos to start. I won't be hungry, but want to watch your technique. You have a maximum of 20 minutes discussing your

romantic past, then it's my turn. We'll stay there until 11:15, at which time we can either leave together or I can pretend to get a call telling my my place is on fire and I'll leave. If I'm still there, we can come back to my place, have sex for 45 minutes, and if you do a good enough job, we can catch a movie Saturday."

Venus in Taurus

Earning the affections of someone with Venus in Taurus can be like trying to pry the lid off the sweetest jar of pickles on the shelf: it's a lot of work, you'll be expected to strain, and (if that lid ever comes off) it's worth the effort. You are fonder of food and material comfort than the average person, and probably have some talent at providing one or the other. Your affections are strong and steady. Venus in Taurus has mastered the art of the cuddle. You have a lot of the qualities that people look for in a mate, which is probably why you tend to be a little lazy in the pursuit of love... you've got the goods, let *them* do the work. You have a good sense of fashion and a bad sense of compromise, so it's important that your mate look good, and look good *with* you.

"Hello gentlemen. I'm an affectionate and caring woman who is seeking her soul mate. I don't particularly care what you do for a living or what you look like, provided you are employed in the financial sector, and are at least a 7.5 out of 10. I would prefer a man who takes care of himself and exercises regularly, as this will help balance out my fondness for anything deep fried. If this sounds interesting, write me today. Also, please send an outline of what you plan for our first date, and a description of the

car you'll pick me up in (no two doors, please!). Race is not important, but I prefer a man who doesn't clash with my new living room set, which I am still paying for."

Venus in Gemini

The way to your heart is probably through the ears: you love nothing better than someone who can express themselves intelligently. That doesn't mean you necessarily fall for "fast talkers" but it happens. A successful relationship requires that someone hone in on exactly what you want out of it, and that covers a lot of ground with you. Your affections are changeable: hyperactively physical one day, and missing in action the next. Although you may not always have great follow-through in your relationships, you are likely a champion flirt. You probably have a lot of friends, and they are likely a source of drama and jealousy, which can be pretty exciting, so you put up with it. Maybe sometimes you even encourage it. After all, "boring" is a fatal sin in a relationship, right?

"Hey guys! I am a wild and spontaneous thrill-seeker and an old fashioned girl all at once. I enjoy extreme sports and staying at home watching a movie. I believe that the greatest sex is exclusively between two people who love each other, preferably while watching one of the videos I made during my amateur porn career. You should dedicated to your career (but not a workaholic), love

children (but not actually want any), and be willing to entertain me when I'm down (or get the hell out of my way, depending on the mood.) And yes... I DO know what I want. Drop me a line now before I get frustrated and remove my ad. Again."

Venus in Cancer

People with Venus in Cancer are sensitive, caring, and easily flustered by signs of distance in your partner. This makes you both a real "catch" and hard to handle. It's a fine line between "a sweetie" and "a sap," and you can usually be found zipping back and forth across that line. You can be demonstrative and physically affectionate, but sometimes require more reassurance that way yourself than your partner is always able to provide. You are particularly fond of having a comfy home (or an exclusive corner of that home) to retreat to, and sometimes luring you out of that cave can be nearly impossible. Even if you don't want any of your own, you are probably great with kids. It can take a lot of work for a potential partner to get past you defences, but you are probably worth the extra effort.

"Greetings. If you are looking for a kind and considerate partner to share the rest of your life with, look no further! I'm looking for someone special to spend quiet quality time with. I want a man who can appreciate a real Woman -- maybe not the flashiest girl out there, but a solid bet for the long term. I am intelligent, witty, charming and attractive, and want to find someone to share my life with.

Send me a message, and if you can find where I live and convince me to come outside (perhaps for chaperoned antique shopping) I could be the girl of your dreams! That is -- if you can find me. I ain't givin' it away."

Venus in Leo

Venus in Leo has an excellent sense for both the high drama and the fun that comes with romance. You love steadiness, praise, and excitement in your love life, like the trophy wife who is always at her millionaire husband's side at all the parties, but quietly maintains a fling with the pool boy. You'd probably get a secret thrill at the notion of someone watching you while you're doing it. Your heart can be hard to win, but you tend to play for keeps. This placement can lead to dramatic jealousy flare-ups, and Venus in Leo sometimes provokes jealousy as a way to reassure itself of its "market value." You may have a talent for acting, which comes in handy when either role-playing in the bedroom or over-emphasizing the details of your anecdotes. Children and small animals appreciate your enthusiastic affection and tolerate your occasional moodiness.

"Dear VetteGuy75: Thank you for writing. Yes, an afternoon at the Water Slide sounds like it would be great fun, but I'm afraid I have a note from my hairdresser prohibiting me from exposure to chlorine. Although you seem like a great guy, I have a couple of questions. First of all, I noticed you are online but are taking an average of twelve minutes to answer

my messages. Are you talking to other women behind my back? How dare you! And I know you're trying to be a gentleman, but those last two pictures I sent you had cleavage in them, and you said nothing. Are you blind? You're not the only guy out there, you know."

Venus in Virgo

Venus in Virgo is often accused of trying to intellectualize their feelings. Having a lot of love to give, you probably find that applying reason helps to cushion the blow in a world full of imperfect people and things to love. People with Venus in Virgo often emit a quiet, high pitched squeal: it's the sound of their intellect trying to keep a grip on their trashy, oversexed side. And (often to the chagrin of your mate) you usually have a really firm grip. People with this placement are often better at showing concern, fretting, and providing quiet advice and/or criticism than producing lavish outbursts of emotion. That's a shame, because there's a lot there, and not everyone enjoys making the effort required to pry you open. You are often a source of sane, caring, quietly judgemental (but still sweet) advice to your loved ones.

"Dear ACowboy42: Thank you for responding to my ad. You certainly seem ruggedly handsome enough, and I like that, but I have a few questions before I meet you. That cold you were complaining about -- what antihistamine are you using? I have a new one that might work better. And, it's certainly exciting that you own a ranch, but shouldn't your wrists be looser when you're cantering? Haven't you trained that horse to use a shank bit

yet? Also, you misspelled "judgemental" in your last response to me. Dinner sounds fine, but I'm allergic to shellfish. Let's make it dinner at your place. Remember: no dairy or peanuts."

Venus in Libra

Venus in Libra is considered to be an excellent placement, making you fond of romance, partnership, sweetness, decorative touches, and compromise. The problem for people involved with you is that it can be hard to see the real you behind all those thoughtful gestures and knick-knacks. You have a particular appreciation for intelligent, well-spoken companions. Venus in Libra appreciates the fine art of debate, but not the bruised feelings that often result. You probably have a good ear for music, a good eye for details, and a hard time passing up a sale. Venus in Libra people are usually kind and understanding with children and small animals, but risk bringing theirs up without enough discipline. Regardless of your looks, the opposite sex probably likes you. And regardless of your numerous past experiences, you probably like them too.

"Hello Men. I am an attractive, intelligent, and charming single lady looking for her Mr. Right. My friends all tell me I'd make a great catch, and I've decided its time to get serious. I have recently graduated with a Bachelor's Degree in Psychology, with an emphasis on Relationship Counselling, and a minor in Food Prep. I'd like to thank all of you who responded to my ad in past. Where did you guys all go after I wrote you back? Did you delete your ads or just block me? Was it

something I said? Why does no one want to get married anymore? This marriage license expires in another two weeks, and I'd hate to have to pay for another one."

Venus in Scorpio

Venus in Scorpio is perhaps best described as "spicy." Lots of people like spicy things, but what they usually expect from Venus is *sweetness*. Thus, romantically, over the long term you can cause a lot of unintentional heartburn. People with this Venus placement have tremendous depth and intensity in their relationships, which can be a good thing in the long term -- or a complete nuisance. You can pull off the "slutty" look better than most. Have you ever seen a nature film of two ants fighting and one gets its head ripped off... but keeps fighting anyway? That head is *you*, when you focus you romantic intentions on someone. As a mate, you bring a lot to the table, and it can be hard to find someone with the energy and focus to play along. You have high emotional standards for your relationships, and may have a hard time finding a mere mortal who can live up to that.

"Dear YoSupDawg: Your ad really caught my attention. You stand out above the other freaks and losers I've seen on this site. You really seem to have it all together, and I like that. About me: I work downtown at a bank and I enjoy playing poker and spending time with my cat in my spare time. There. Now that you've gotten to know me a little better, we should meet this weekend. Clear your calendar. I have you Thursday evening until Sunday afternoon. we'll

start with dinner. We can split the bill, and then I take over for the remainder of the date. Tell your friends you're going to be 'tied up' for the rest of the weekend. No, that wasn't a figure of speech."

Venus in Sagittarius

You probably love the "chase" stage of a romance, and usually start new relationships with enthusiasm and a sense of adventure. The sense of adventure for your partner often comes at the end of the relationship, when you've given in to the impulse to wander off somewhere else just as they've decided it's time to commit. This is because you have very high ideals as to what a relationship should be, and enjoy the process and sport of romance... thus odds are good you've probably had more than your fair share of them and you recognize that there are "plenty of fish" out there willing to play along. You probably enjoy some form of friendly competition. Unfortunately your partner may often find he/she has to compete for your attention with your friends, family, and hobbies. People with Venus in Sagittarius are easy to forgive for their relationship blunders, which is a good thing, because they have plenty of them.

"Woo hoo! Hey dudes, this sporty little gal is here for a good time, not a long time. A lot of women are here looking to get married or have a baby, but guys... I'm just like you. I'm here for one thing and one thing only. I need it, and I need it bad, and I need it from a real man. I'm tired of taking care of my needs all by myself. Do you think you have what it takes? Can you go for hours without a break? Can you find that

magic spot and sink it the first time, every time? Do you swing a big club? If so, let's meet up and get it going. This girl hasn't played Mini Golf in ages, and I want to kick your ass at it. All night long, baby. You bring the pencil, and I'll keep the score. And no, none of that was a metaphor."

Venus in Capricorn

People with Venus in Capricorn are solid, reliable, affectionate, caring, and involved partners, once you've correctly filled in all the paperwork to get to their heart. Finances can get in the way of any relationship, but you probably respond to (real or imagined) financial threats a little worse than most. You don't object to a significant age difference in a relationship if the person is "the right one" (or as close as you are likely to get in an imperfect world). Venus in Capricorn doesn't usually engage in blatant public displays of affection, but can get good and freaky with it in private. You can project an air of calm stability to your partners, which is often misleading. Generally you are considered to be "a solid bet" for a relationship. Relationships can be a lot of work, but you don't mind doing it as much as most would.

"Gentlemen: I am seeking a committed long-term relationship. Is that what you are looking for? Are you wanting to jump right into a commitment? Are you allergic to cats? Do you enjoy long walks on the beach? Do you have a reasonable balance of stocks and bonds in your investment portfolio? Are you patient? Are you intelligent? Will my friends find

anything about you to make fun of? Do you enjoy being questioned at length if you've done something to make me suspicious? Will you avoid checking out any other women when we're on a date? If you've made it this far in my ad and said 'no' to any of the above, you've already wasted my time and yours."

Venus in Aquarius

Venus in Aquarius likes to think it's in tune with some kind of Universal Love Vibration, and they often are. Of course, that can just be a nice way of saying "you are tough to pin down in a long-term relationship." You probably have some unusual tastes in art, entertainment, and sex... and often treat sex as if it were a form of art and/or entertainment. It *is*, but your partners often wish you'd come across as more deeply emotionally involved. Venus in Aquarius people are prone to sudden, unusual attractions than often sputter out quickly, leaving your partners confused. You are unlikely to let age, status, race, religion, or common sense dictate who you become involved with. Venus in Aquarius has the strange appeal of an exotic bird, and is just as hard to keep happily caged in the long term. If your lover can't also be your friend, then they probably don't stand a chance with you.

"Dear SmalltownFlyGuy: I wasn't sure if I'd respond to your ad until I saw the picture of you at the barbeque. There is nothing sexier than a man with a grill. And the shot of you getting the costume award at the science fiction convention was incredibly hot too. According to your interests, you read. So do I! We have so much in common! I'd love to meet you for coffee

and go from there. I think we have real potential to click, and I'm told it's time I settled down. And is that your room mate in that last picture? He's pretty cute. He looks familiar -- I think I may have dated him a few months ago. Bring him along too, I'm in a weird mood and I get bored quickly."

Venus in Pisces

Pisces is possibly the strongest position in the Zodiac for Venus to be in, and people with that placement usually exemplify the finest Venusian qualities: loving, caring, creative, and compassionate. These qualities are often favorite targets for con men and heartbreakers, and your loving, compassionate handling of them doesn't exactly help. You have a real capacity to empathize with others, and often rely on that rather than using logic. Since you have a lot of love to give, you've probably been cheated in this department more than once, and may be hesitant to get back up on that horse again. Nonetheless you are appealing enough that someone, eventually, will likely talk you into it. Relationships aren't usually very hard work for you, which is good, because you don't like hard work. Your kindness and empathy mean that in any relationship, *you* are likely to be the one doing most of the emotional heavy lifting.

"Dear Dreamerman: When I first saw your ad, I knew we were meant to be together throughout eternity. I know you've never had the love you deserved, but I am here to make that all better. And when you responded to my first message, that just confirmed it to me. Yes, I'd love to meet you for a few drinks. Any of the

places you mentioned would be fine. If you buy the first round, I will let you name the babies. I'm so excited! I've never met anyone as amazing as you! One more question, though: it's hard to tell with the beard, but aren't you my ex-husband Dave? And what are you doing out of rehab so soon?"

Dress For Success
Working Your Venus Sign To Maximum Effect

(This section is addressed specifically for women... although the same kind of advice works for you too, except when applied to your Mars placement instead of Venus. Men, you get your own Seduction Tips at the end of the Mars section. And, ladies? The Mars advice -- applied to a man's Venus placement -- works just fine for you too.)

You already know far better than I do what colors and kind of outfits look better on you than I do. But there are a few suggestions that can go a long way towards maximizing your sexiness. These are all based on your Venus placement, which is an indicator of how your specific feminine charms work. Here are a few suggestions that may compliment your current look and get you more compliments in general.

Aries: Think "sporty." This placement tends to look good casual. Looking like you're on your way to the gym or at least ready for movement works well for you.

Taurus: Add a soft and feminine accent to whatever you'd normally wear, like a lacy bra strap that pops out at random moments. Think "old fashioned girl with modern attitude."

Gemini: Add interesting details, like earrings with a complex design or a jingly anklet. Just as your conversation sparkles, so should you, a little.

Cancer: Comfortable textures and materials look good on you, even if no one is actually touching you at the moment. A lot of men like the classic angora sweater and angora like *you*, too.

Leo: Add a little dramatic flair to whatever you've decided to wear, like big hoop earrings or a dangly necklace that casually points to your cleavage.

Virgo: Think "naughty librarian." Believe it or not, you really can pull off that (mostly) prim and proper look, with just one detail that hints that the façade can be made to vanish quickly.

Libra: Pretty and girly. You were born to work the summer dress and the floral accents. You already have a good sense of style – individualize it with a creative accessory.

Scorpio: Spicy! You've probably already been told to go with red or black. That isn't necessary – but even one strategically-placed fire-engine red accent will really light a fire.

Sagittarius: No one can pull off the t-shirt and jeans look like you can! Anything that looks casual (and looks like it can be removed quickly) will work well on you.

Capricorn: Pretend you're getting dressed for work, and you work as a loan officer. Except instead of approving access to money, you're approving access to you. One pricey item can pull it all together.

Aquarius: be entirely comfortable within yourself, and whatever you wear – and add something a little unusual or showy, like rings on each finger or complex Peruvian-style earrings.

Pisces: Go with a soft and dreamy look – think romance novel, or hippie chick. A little bit of glitter can go a long way with you. And make sure you're drawing attention to your eyes.

Mars - Hot And Bothered

Mars is where you get your bollocks from. Named after the God of War, the Red Planet has been a popular source of fictional invaders over the years, and that's appropriate: Mars has a lot to do with your drives, your ambitions, and your temper. Mars also has a lot to do with your sex drive. People who have strong Mars placements in their birth charts with a lot of difficult aspects to it tend to be competitive, oversexed, or just plain obnoxious. It's also where you get a lot of your drive in general from, so without it you wouldn't really get anything done. Of course, all of these negative attributes are also prime qualities of the typical Space Hero who shows up to drive off the Martian invaders. That may not be the sort of behavior you'd welcome at your next dinner party, but you've got to admit that sometimes it's good to have a Space Hero around.

Mars also rules processes involving heat and cutting implements, like cooking. That's why I've turned this chapter over to famous TV chef Gordon Ramsay, who will give you his personal opinion of the pros and cons of Mars through each sign in the birth chart... presented "Hell's Kitchen" style. Well, let's be honest... this is Gordon Ramsay, so it's mostly cons. (Also, these aren't *real* Gordon Ramsay quotes, but I have a lot of soft aspects to my Mars, so I tend to get my results by being quiet and a little under-handed.)

Mars in Aries

Mars is strong in Aries, and the head-first attitude of The Ram suits it well. People with this placement are usually energetic and strong-willed. You likely launch into new projects with great enthusiasm, but may get too easily bored or distracted when the grind hits. Mars in Aries isn't always terribly organized with its time or energy, but often achieves its goals anyway. You are likely a fierce competitor, able to completely lose yourself in a game or in achieving your goals. Whether you are athletic or not, you'd probably be a great cheerleader (literally or figuratively). Your temper may flare up quickly, but it usually burns out quickly too. People with Mars in Aries tend to be hell on wheels in bed, until they become bored, at which time they are at least as useless as everyone else is. They also have a strange tendency to bump their heads more than most other people -- a spin-off effect of being naturally "headstrong."

"Bloody awful. You were in too much of a hurry and the grill was overheated. You started cooking the chicken kebabs before anyone had actually ordered. You're not a f--king chef, you're a pyromaniac with an apron."

Mars in Taurus

Mars in Taurus is not considered to be a great placement, but you are too stubborn to let that stop you. Like a bull, you are probably placid most of the time, until something provokes your temper -- at which time you become a raging menace that's almost impossible to stop. You probably have some kind of creative talent, whether you are using it or not. You were probably a star in kindergarten when it came to arts and crafts -- and that was probably the last time you were able to work for a long stretch of time without being distracted by thoughts of material gain or sex. When your drives are frustrated, you are more likely than the average person to treat your problem with food. You tend to be practical and methodical in your approach to problem-solving, and have a great deal of energy to get things done -- you just have a hard time *engaging* that drive. You probably like sex a little more than the average person, are probably a little better at it than the average, and you'd probably get a lot more of it if you were better at getting up off the couch and going to get some.

"It took you twenty f--king minutes to grill the bass. It came out tough, so you turn

the heat up when I corner you about it and burn the steak. Do you even know what you're doing here?"

Mars in Gemini

Mars in Gemini loves directing its aggression and sense of adventure into verbal and intellectual situations, where aggression and a sense of adventure aren't often welcome. You favorite way to resolve a conflict with a loved one is usually with a solid verbal assault, followed by a few sharp verbal stings, and finishing up with mild confusion as to why everyone wants to walk on eggshells to avoid provoking your anger. Much of your anger and aggression seems to start with minor incorrect details or logical inconsistencies, which you secretly can't stand. People with Mars in Gemini often have better than average mechanical ability, or better than average ability to figure out where that extra park in the do-it-yourself furniture kit is supposed to go, and/or whether or not the thing will stand on its own without it. You have a good sex drive, but it can be a little fickle and unpredictable. Teach your mate to talk dirty and it will help with this.

"Don't try to talk your way out of this: the filet is damned near raw on one side and burned on the other. Ever heard of a little f--cking thing called 'consistency of effort'?"

Mars in Cancer

This is perhaps the trickiest placement for Mars; you have just as much drive and aggression as anyone else, but have more difficulty expressing it properly. People with Mars in Cancer are more prone than others to suppressing their anger, and ultimately pointing it inwards; resulting in high blood pressure, ulcers, and sometimes even gagging when sufficiently angry. That's because you are sufficiently sensitive to the feelings of others around you that you realize that lashing out really does hurt people... and you don't like that. You'd have more of a reputation as a sex bomb if your considerable drive wasn't linked to your fluctuating moods, making you look kind of fickle to your partners. Any natural shyness or inhibitions you may have will eventually go away once you are in a genuinely caring, supportive relationship. Once you are past the childhood issues you were handed (and you were), you will make an excellent parent.

"The Beef Wellington is undercooked and you tried to hide it with sauce, and you managed to burn your finger doing it. You can't be a chef if you're afraid of the f--king grill or hurting the meat's feelings."

Mars in Leo

You have a lot of energy and were probably told at one point or another you should consider a career in acting... or at least that you should contain your flare for the dramatic when you are angry. You are good at initially tackling an issue, and have enough follow-through to take most of the credit when a practical solution is finally found. You are straightforward and enthusiastic in your passions, and once you have a romantic target in your sights you can be unstoppable. You don't take well to being spurned -- many stalkers have Mars in Leo. You can get away with stalking more than the average person, because once you've worn 'em down, you make it worth their while in bed. You have an appealing, almost child-like nature when you are enthusiastic about something. This means you should probably spend more time playing with your dog and less time "helping" your co-workers, which they often perceive as you attempting to hog the limelight.

"You turned a simple stir-fry into a f--king flambé. Burning your initials onto the green peppers was a nice touch -- or would be if it was f--king cufflinks you were cooking, not lunch. All presentation, no substance. Bloody awful."

Mars in Virgo

Mars in Virgo isn't prone to getting its way with sudden flare-ups: this placement would much rather approach its goals in a thorough, consistent way. This would qualify you to be an excellent surgeon and a terrible nag as a mate. You do thorough, detailed work, which your boss likes -- and which means you'll likely get promoted into management, where you will become a micromanaging, nitpicking nuisance to everyone else. Often too compassionate and passive, Mars in Virgo frequently takes out its worries and repressed frustrations on its own digestive tract. You are more likely to blow up over an accumulation of small issues rather than attacking the one big problem directly. Your sexual partners probably have great things to say about you, provided you've been able to overcome your performance anxiety, which you were born with -- probably needlessly.

"I love the way you've perfectly cubed the onions here. The flavors in the sauce are perfectly balanced. Next time, though, try not waiting three hours for the skillet to get to exactly the right f--king temperature. The customers left."

Mars in Libra

Mars in Libra has a strong urge to apply its energies to social situations and friendships, and is usually pleasant enough about it that no one realizes you're being bossy until you've gotten your way and everyone is going for Indonesian food like you wanted. You usually handle social situations well, and often make a good party better simply by showing up. You tend to get annoyed at social slights and rudeness than the average person. Mars in Libra people tend to fantasize about growing up and getting married at a younger age than the other kids, and are as surprised as anyone else (maybe more so) when it falls through the first time. Your natural urge to be noticed and appreciated for your gifts can make you talented in the bedroom, with a camera, and possibly with both at the same time.

"Beautiful presentation. Great use of local ingredients. Utterly f--king bland, though. You've tried too hard not to offend my palate, and you've ended up wasting my f--king time."

Mars in Scorpio

Be careful to choose the targets of your anger carefully: your fury is a powerful thing, and could easily take out a couple of innocent bystanders. You're probably just as afraid of death in an emergency as the next guy, but are much less likely to show it. This Mars placement has a reputation for being vengeful and unswerving, which just means you should have killed all your enemies sooner so they wouldn't badmouth you. No matter how many relationships you've had, and regardless of the nature of the break-up, it's unlikely any of your exes are complaining about the sex: you're good at it, and you know it. It's more likely that your jealousy and possessiveness broke it up. When you hold someone close, they know it, and when you hold a grudge, *everyone* knows it.

"F--k me, think you've spiced that enough? I can't taste anything else over the f--cking cayenne. It's completely drowned out the other ingredients. Work with the food, not against it."

Mars in Sagittarius

Mars in Sagittarius enjoys starting up games, spots, and philosophical arguments. You might well be suited to a career in the military, despite the fact that normally people have a hard time telling you what to do. You have a strong idealistic streak, and easily rise to the occasion when there is a larger principle that needs to be defended. Mars in Sagittarius people need to keep moving, and will often lapse into depression if they don't make getting out and staying busy a priority. You are a fierce fighter, but usually play fair. People with Mars in Sagittarius tend to treat sex like it's a sport. This can be a good thing (in that it makes you want to improve your score) and a bad thing (because your partner may sense it's just a game to you). Regardless of your experience level, you are a quick and enthusiastic student.

"You overcooked a salad! A f--king salad! That's what happens when you try to cook nine things at once. And did you even open a cook book? That raw veal ought to be a big f--king hit with the customers."

Mars in Capricorn

Mars in Capricorn is focused, intense, and efficient. This is generally considered to be the "best" Mars placement, as feisty Mars benefits from Capricorn's sense of self-control. You likely don't lose your temper quickly or loudly. When you put your mind to it, however, you can be incredibly vengeful and are willing to wait as long as it takes for the perfect moment to strike. You like to be given clear-cut, practical guidance at work and in your relationships, which tends to be good for one and no so romantic for the other. Mars in Capricorn uses its energy efficiently, but can't stand "laziness" in others. You are warm and affectionate with the ones you love, but can easily turn it off like a switch when they've hurt or disappointed you. Once you are focused on a goal, you are likely to achieve it, regardless of who or what has to be bulldozed to get to it.

"Orderly presentation, everything cooked properly and on time. Nothing burnt. Excellent job. Except, of course, this isn't a f--king McDonald's. It's called 'panache,' look it the f--k up."

Mars in Aquarius

The surest way to annoy someone with Mars in Aquarius is to tie them down, restrict them, or (worst of all) keep insisting that you stick to protocol. You are generally good at applying your intelligence to solving practical problems, even if your solutions sometimes look a little weird to everyone else. People with this placement like to apply their energies to changing and reforming existing structures and procedures to make them more fair and work better, and are often surprised when this isn't welcome. You are generally a lot of fun and fair-minded in your relationships, and in your bedroom. Mars in Aquarius people usually have a reasonably good grip on their tempers and passions, which is usually a good thing -- but can make you seem a little detached and impersonal to your loved ones.

"I have to admit I'm surprised. Perfectly cooked tenderloin, nice job on the coating, not too greasy. Good job on the onions too. Perfect. Too bad the customers ordered the f--king sea bass, you moron!"

Mars in Pisces

Mars is a little too belligerent to be entirely comfortable in the sensitive sign of Pisces. People with this placement have powerful emotions and passions, and often have a hard time keeping them under control. You may find yourself misdirecting your energies into the wrong person and the wrong project, which can make you a versatile lover and employee -- or can find you unemployed and alone. You probably aren't terribly comfortable with directly attacking a problem or issue, and will often sit around and wait until things correct themselves. Fortunately, this happens just often enough that you can keep justifying it to yourself. Sometimes people with Mars in Pisces find the best use of their energy is in helping others, or in pursuing artistic, creative, or socially beneficial goals. More than most, you understand that the best sex involves a healthy dose of love.

"Well, you almost got it right. You started out great with the appetizers, but by the time we got to the main courses you empathized with the cutlets so much you couldn't braise them. And stop crying. Real chefs don't f--king cry."

Take Action:
Working Your Mars On A First Date

(Since Mars rules the sex drive, and action in general, and since men are traditionally the ones who ask for that first date, this information is here and directed towards men. However, the same advice – especially directed at a man's Venus sign – works just as well, regardless of gender.)

How you get the ball rolling with someone romantically often depends on the activities on a first date. Getting the mind and/or body working is the first step to getting a relationship to work. When you're asking a woman for a date, try basing the activity in question on her Mars placement. What's well begun is half done

Aries: If this lady has any interest in sports, sporting events, or competition at all, this can really get her going. Even a game of darts at your local pub can do it.

Taurus: Dinner and drinks is, of course, the classic first date and this advice applies twice as much in this case. Pick somewhere a little on the high end, both price- and calorie-wise.

Gemini: Any chance to observe and comment and exchange ideas will be a winner. A movie (but a well-reviewed one) or a perch at the coffee shop to people-watch both work well.

Cancer: Think "water" and "comfort": two things that will put your date at ease. Seafood at a place with particularly comfy seating, or a movie an older, cosy theater work well.

Leo: Whatever you do, keep in mind where your eyes should be during the date on your date, not anywhere else. So, dinner or dancing, yes. Staring at a movie screen? No. Save that for next time.

Virgo: Stimulate your date's mind. People-watching, lectures, and live performances are all excellent choices. **Libra**: Think music, comfort, and creativity. This placement has an appreciation for the arts and the little personal touches. A stroll past a hand-crafted ethnic jewellery stand at the mall works like a charm.

Scorpio: Don't be afraid to go a little exotic with it. Even if you don't go dancing, going somewhere involving a strong, rhythmic beat will do you wonders.

Sagittarius: Don't just go to a restaurant go to something exotic. Why bother with Chinese *again*, when there's a new Tibetan place that's just opened up?

Capricorn: In many ways, it's hard to go wrong with this one if you handle it traditionally. Go unique, but not startling and whatever you do, *you pay the tab.*

Aquarius: New and unique is the way to go. Don't be afraid to be a little odd, offbeat or even silly. When's the last time you tried mini-golf or pottery painting?

Pisces: The activity isn't as important as the vibe surrounding it. Pisces is sensitive to their environment. Don't just go to a restaurant

Part Four
The Compatibility Guides

The final section of this book consists of the Compatibility Guides from my blog. Yes, it's all Sun Sign stuff and yet, it's *more.* Armed with the information in this book, the compatibility factors can be applied to your Moon Signs(s) and the placement of your personal planets.

For example: suppose your Sun Sign is Pisces, and your sweetie is a Cancer. You look at what everyone has to say about that combination, and you'd think everything ought to be fine. But suppose your Moon is in Taurus, and your partner's moon is in Sagittarius? We've established that for emotional relationships that the Moon is at least as important as the Sun so this would explain why it is you want to stay at home and snuggle, and your Significant Other is always insisting on taking you skydiving or night clubbing. And suppose everything works Sun and Moon-wise but your Mercury is in Aries and your loved one has Mercury in Cancer. No wonder the conversation breaks down! Or, your Mars is in Virgo and your partner has theirs in Aquarius. That's why your sex drives are on different pages half the time. And so on

Knowing your Sign Placements, and those of others you are (or have been) involved with, have a look through the Compatibility Guides. You'll be surprised at how easily these otherwise complex matters can fall into place.

And remember: no one is perfect; therefore there can be no perfect relationships. And besides sometimes it's the *differences* that can lend a relationship its real strength and beauty

Love Is A Battlefield
The Aries Compatibility Guide

As much as a cliché as it might be, I still find that when an Aries approaches me about their love life, the question may be "Is so-and-so my soul mate?" or "Should I continue to pursue whatshisface?"...but the *real* question is "how much of a fight am I going to have to put up to get things right?" But you want romance, and whether you're a man or a woman, you love the challenge.

I've decided to demonstrate Aries compatibility by showing you how easy or hard the planned Aries invasion of Love Island will be, based on the sign of the partner.

THE BEACH: The Fire signs, **Aries, Leo and Sagittarius**. Flat, level terrain here with little resistance. Another Aries might seem like the logical place to start. Trouble probably will set in when your next planned combat action isn't on the same path as your partner's. Leo is comfortable, but they can be less goal-oriented than you. That can be frustrating. Sagittarius is a pleasant fit, but you may have this nagging feeling they aren't taking you seriously enough. And you're probably right.

THE GRASSLANDS: The Air signs, **Gemini, Libra, and Aquarius**. A little more work to empathize with, but still relatively easy to reach. Only the occasionally spear is thrown at you as you approach. Gemini can be a little more scattered and indecisive than you. Aquarius can be similarly passionate about things, yet strangely dispassionate about them too, and that can be frustrating. Libra is a little further inland and hilly, but worth the extra travel. You may find the natives here react to your every strategic move, making them surprisingly hard to catch off guard for such nice people.

MOUNT BULLMORE: **Taurus**. Lush fields protected by stubborn thick jungle and a steep climb. This one will take some time to achieve, but may well be worth it as a stabilizing influence. Watch out for the vines: they cling. *Hard.*

DREAMY VALLEY: **Pisces**. Gentle, restful, green and luscious. It's a shame you have to go through so much damned work just to find a place to rest. And the terrain here can be confusing and unclear. Is that a good thing or a bad thing? You decide.

FLINTY RIDGE: **Virgo**. On the face of it, you two have neither nothing in common nor any reason for conflict. This can actually be a great place for you to camp out. All you'll have to do is convince the natives it's okay. And do it in their language, not yours. Good luck with that.

SCORPION PASS: Remember that great scene in "The Fellowship Of The Ring" where Gandalf held off the giant Balrog in a spectacular battle, only for both of them to plunge to their deaths? Yes, one of them did come back for the next movie. You think that's you, or **Scorpio**? It's a coin toss. You like those odds?

THE DEFENSIVE MOUNTAINS: **Cancer and Capricorn**. You wouldn't leave your valuables in the driveway and lock up your old newspapers, would you? These two are emotionally defensive because they have a lot going on inside, and they are the most reactive to a sudden jab. The problem here is that "sudden jab" is your style, whether you like it or not.

So why even bother? I don't have to tell you. You're an Aries. It's all about the *victory*, baby... glorious, glorious victory.

Sowing The Seeds Of Love
The Taurus Guide To Compatibility

A Taurus, whether a man or a woman, has a reputation for not rushing into things. Of course when the heart calls, a Taurus responds just as quickly as anyone else. But how to nurture that relationship properly and how to tell what kind of an emotional investment you've made? Will it be delicious, beautiful... or just a weed?

Here's a handy guide to your relationships, Taurus, based on how much work you'll have to put into them. Even the hardiest perennials need some tending, and even the most difficult patch of soil can be made to sprout something beautiful. But some of those patches of soil are a *lot* easier to work than others...

RICH, DARK SOIL: The other Earth signs (**Virgo and Capricorn**), Cancer, and Pisces. These spots in the garden aren't going to need a lot of tending. Rich in emotion, yet cautious like you. A good long-term investment of your time and energy. Virgo may not always show as much blossom as you like, Capricorn sometimes has trouble taking root deeply, and Pisces tends to wander all over like a vine. Cancer has good tenacity, but needs encouragement to sprout.

FERTILE, BUT REQUIRES A LOT OF TENDING: Another **Taurus or Scorpio**. You'll probably have fun with these, but they're going to take more work than the average. Another Taurus may sound like a natural, but they can be as stubborn as you, and do you need more of that? Scorpio brings some dynamic blooms, but you may find it leeches too many nutrients from your soil.

SHADY, REQUIRES EXTRA FERTILIZER: **Libra and Sagittarius**. Like you, Libra is a Venus-ruled sign. This should make the two of you perfect, but Libra needs more attention than you might be ready to give it. As for Sagittarius: it's not the sort of thing you'd ever actually plan on planting, on the face of it... but it seems to work anyway. Bright foliage makes up for all the weeding and wandering into the neighbor's plot.

REQUIRES INTENSIVE WATERING: **Aries and Gemini**. These astrological neighbors can be appealing, but take a lot more work than most for you to maintain. Aries is always looking for a hotter climate to sprout in, and Gemini puts down its roots where you want them to go... and everywhere else, too. Neither one takes well to being pruned. A TOUGH ROW TO HOE: **Leo and Aquarius**. Leo can make a flamboyant centerpiece to any garden. It's just that their wild impulsive growth spurts make them hard to manage, and the huge blooms distract from why you wanted a garden in the first place. Aquarius, like you, grows at its own pace, but you may end up accidentally fertilizing it to death trying to make it grow your way... something Aquarius just won't do.

No matter what relationship you find yourself in, there will be work. And there will be rewards. And as these things go, Taurus, some clichés are true. In romance, you really do have a green thumb!

Should I Stay Or Should I Go?
The Gemini Guide To Compatibility

Welcome back to the exciting final round of "Should I Stay, Or Should I Go?"

Today's contestant, Gemini, is on the verge of walking away with the Grand Prize... true love! Now Gemini, all you have to do is answer one question correctly. The cash value of the question represents the degree of difficulty involved. Naturally, you might want to pick an easier Sign... but playing it safe all the time didn't get you as far as it has.

LIBRA ($200): If someone wants to go the same direction you want to go, but you're always going in two different directions at once, can *they* keep up?

AQUARIUS ($200): There's no question that you can be cool and dispassionate when you want to, knowing your partner will appreciate the affection when it comes later. But what if your partner has a chill schedule of his/her own?

ARIES ($400): If a train leaves Chicago traveling east at 50 miles per hours, and you want to go west, are you going to end up *under* this train instead of *on* it?

LEO ($400): If fun and passionate meet materialistic and possessive in a dark back alley, who will win the knife fight? And are *you* the darkened back alley?

SAGITTARIUS ($400): If two freedom fighters team up, and one of them changes flags every other day, how long until the two freedom fighters end up shooting each other, even if it's by accident?

GEMINI ($600): If two people manage to travel in four directions at once, will either of them end up getting *anywhere* together, or *everywhere*?

VIRGO ($600): Emotionally, is X greater than Y, if Y equals Virgo? Solve for X. Having fun yet? Didn't think so. It's supposed to be a *romance*, not a math problem.

TAURUS ($800): If slow and steady wins the race, will you get tired of the prize and want to take up poker before you get to the finish line if you're riding a Bull?

CAPRICORN ($800): If a hot air balloon has a relative weight of -50 pounds, how many boulders will a Capricorn pile on to ground it until the balloon turns into just an empty bag that doesn't fly?

CANCER ($800): Which lasts longer: Cancer's ability to dive deep into the dark waters of over-emotionality, or your ability to hold your breath while they drag you down with them?

SCORPIO ($1000): How many times per day do you need to be told to mentally and verbally "get to the point" before you trade in your honeymoon tickets to Hawaii for a bus ticket to Anywhere But Here?

PISCES ($1000): (Two part question) 1) A bird may love a fish, but where would they live? 2) How long will it take two birds to either eat two fish, or drown?

Go ahead, Gemini... pick a Grand Prize question. Or, if you prefer, just spin the wheel. That approach seems to work for you too...

Miss Crabtree's Old-Fashioned Grade Six Schoolmarm Guide To Cancer

Compatibility Hello, children, I'm Miss Crabtree, your Compatibility teacher this semester. We're going to do things a little differently this year. I'm going to be handing out your grades at the *start* of the class, based on how easy or difficult it's going to be for me to get along with you. *Stop fidgeting, Leo!* You can bring your mark up with hard work. I'm not going to just hand any of you a passing grade. Okay... I just did that with most of you. *Spit that gum out, Capricorn!* I'm sure I'll enjoy this experience with all of you though, and so will you. Otherwise, you can take your sass to the Principal's office.

Scorpio and Pisces: You pay attention in class and work well with me. Scorpio, you have a real tenacity that I appreciate, especially when it comes to me. Excellent note-taking. Watch the frustration with the tougher tests, though. And Pisces, you are just so sweet! Always a joy to have in class. Try to borrow some of Scorpio's focus though, would you? Your attention is drifting too much. A+

Taurus and Virgo: You're both solid, determined and reliable. You always get to class on time. Taurus, I really like your affection and sensuality, but your stubborn resistance to learning new material lost you a mark. Try harder. Virgo: nice job of showing all your work on the test papers. But could you please try to look like you're enjoying being here more than you do? More enthusiasm, please. **A**

Capricorn: You're a good solid student. My only problem is that this is *Relationship* class. Close your History text... I know there's a test in an hour, but your eyes are supposed to be on me now.*Me.* Less seriousness, more involvement here please. **B+**

Leo: Honestly, I don't understand why you're here at all. You never focus, you're always clowning around, and it's very distracting. Good thing for you we find each other inexplicably adorable. Should I spell "inexplicable" for you? Your spelling is criminally sloppy. **B**

Gemini: Improvement needed. Your brightness always contributes to the class, but I have this strange insecure feeling you're always looking out the window at the playground when my back is turned. And sit up straight! And turn off the IPod when I'm talking to you! **C+**

Sagittarius: You walk in here like *you're* the teacher. Well... you aren't. *I am.* Quit grinning at me like that! Are you taking this seriously? You're always fun to have around at recess, though. It's too bad that "recess" doesn't count for any of your final mark. **C-**

Aquarius: Listen, Aquarius. This is an elective course. Quit acting like you're here because of a court order! You look like you're taking notes, but with that shiny new laptop of yours, you could just as easily be playing games on there. Have you heard a single thing I've said here? **C-**

Cancer: I'm too defensive? No, *you're* too defensive! I feel like I'm talking to a brick wall with you sometimes. What do you mean, "*I'm* the brick wall?" *That does it.* Go to the Principal's office. There's only room enough here for *my* crabbiness. **D**

Aries: Aries? Aries? Has anyone here seen Aries today? Oh, there you are out on the playground. Aries, get in here!! Yes, it's time for Relationship class. No, *you're* watch isn't right, *mine* is. It's not time for PE. What? *What did you just call me, you little...?* **D**

Libra: You're so sweet, and you normally excel at this class. Bringing me the apple was a nice touch. But when I correct you, that is no excuse for a crying jag that disrupts the entire class. And no I'm not an "insensitive jerk" with you, Libra. Yes, I *saw* that note you passed Aquarius! You're normally so good at this class, but I'm not seeing any proof of effort on your part at all. I require *effort!* **F**

Overture, Curtain Lights
The Leo Guide To Compatibility

Welcome to the twelve-screen multiplex of Love. Today we're going to see if we can successfully hook our friend Leo up with the man/woman/movie of his/her/its dreams. And if you're a true movie fan, you know that the right review from the right critic can improve your chance of being really entertained... despite the sticky floor and overpriced popcorn. Of course, even your favorite film critic can get it wrong once in a while... and what's more fun than uncovering an under appreciated cinematic gem?

Tickets, please...

NOW SHOWING:

Blaze Of Love (**Aries and Sagittarius**): Action! Suspense! Romance! This one has it all. Aries can't help but overact a little, and Sagittarius is all exuberance and no technique, but with a little editing this one could have been perfect. Big thumbs up! **FIVE STARS.**

C'est Moi, Mon Amour (**Leo**): An intense and compelling tale with few flaws. The main flaw here is that the romantic leads keep acting like it's just their movie. A bit sappy for some people's tastes. **FOUR STARS.**

The Mirror Has Two Faces (**Gemini and Libra**): Playful and romantic. The fast-paced but occasionally erratic screenplay keeps things moving at a furious clip. The perfect way to while away an evening. Occasionally thin characterization leaves some doubt as to whether or not the energy can be maintained for the planned sequels. **THREE AND A HALF STARS.**

I Married A Martian (**Aquarius**): An obscure yet compelling opening leads the audience into a wonderland of surprises, romance, and culture clashes. The director's detached approach can be frustrating for the summer-romance-movie crowd. The special effects are amazing, but at times you'll crave the human element more. **THREE AND A HALF STARS.**

Pinchy And The Drain (**Cancer**): This fish-out-of-water comedy/romance/buddy movie works better than you might expect. The film bogs down at about the two-thirds point in maudlin sentimentality. Affectionate, wants to reach out to the audience, but at times you'll wonder about character motivation, and not necessarily in a good way. **THREE STARS.**

The Sting III - Ouch! (**Scorpio**): A confused tale of a carefree organ-grinder's monkey and the researcher who loves it, yet wants to dissect it. The two are strangely compelled to each other, and it all plays out in a painfully predictable ending. PETA protested on opening night, and you may too before it's over. Warning: extreme gore. **TWO AND A HALF STARS.**

Warm Heart, Clean Fish (**Virgo and Pisces**): This tale of an obsessive-compulsive fishmonger and an alcoholic marine biologist starts out promising. Sometimes when a director juxtaposes two incompatible characters it's a classic buddy movie; this one's just all wet. Sweet, but never seems to really gel into a coherent storyline. **TWO AND A HALF STARS.**

Pamplona Or Bust (**Taurus**): Slow-paced and frustrating, yet packed with explosions and car chases. This film knows what it wants right from the opening credits and won't let go, which is not necessarily a good thing. You'll wonder what karma made you pick this instead of one of the comedies. A tale told by an idiot, full of sound and fury; signifying nothing. **TWO STARS.**

Death On A Glacier (**Capricorn**): Challenging and surprisingly complex. Not for the faint of heart. This one is a tough climb right from the start. The director seems unsympathetic to his characters, yet there is a point to it all. You just may have a hard time sitting through 90 minutes of frozen wasteland and flat dialogue to get to it. **ONE STAR.**

Of course, all decent movies have a character overcoming some challenge or another. And this cineplex offers twelve screens full of challenges, each different. Besides, you love movies. Even the bad ones, sometimes...

The Virgo Guide To Compatibility, Within A Tolerance of ± 0.2 Millimeters

INITIAL CONDITIONS:
Humans are driven by biosocial factors to pair-bonding. Further, the efficiency of each bond ("compatibility") is variable with each individual involved, in part due to personality-based initial conditions ("Sign"). Virgo attempts to place this within a rational context and draw accurate conclusions.

HYPOTHESIS:
Virgo can find true love within the confines of an imperfect world. Based on broad personality data gathered by Sign, it is projected that the relative probability of success in a pair-bond can thus be projected on an *a priori* basis. Each potential partner is evaluated on a scale of 0 to 1 as a function of probable incidence of harmony (on a per incidence basis).

DATA:
Taurus and Capricorn (0.8/1): Perform well under stress; high tensile shear resistance. Partner malleability is occasionally impaired when reconfiguration is required. Reconfiguration will likely be proposed based on their data set, not yours.

With practice, subject will experience excellent subject conformity to relationship guidelines.

Cancer and Scorpio (0.75/1): Both require some cleaning. Generally sound emotional depth, but both filter their data via emotional factors more than Virgo, and can be resistant to probing. Hardened shells may be difficult to open, but can reward the effort. Emotional slipperiness can occur. Wear rubber gloves.

Pisces (0.7): Highly sensitive to contamination, like yourself. Highly suggestible, unlike yourself. A lack of detail and definition can be frustrating to the researcher; however, emotional appeal can be highly catalytic. A great deal of net-casting is often needed to collect accurate emotional data.

Sagittarius and Virgo (0.65/1): Both signs demonstrate a sympathetic knowledge for further life data, but are likely to use entirely different experimental models than the researcher, making for potential translation problems. Theoretically shouldn't work, but often does anyway. This requires further research.

Aries and Aquarius (0.6/1): Difficult, volatile substances which come with certain containment hazards. One is highly explosive, the other is often too neutral to form a reaction. However, once proper procedures are in place, this can (paradoxically) make long term bonding possible. Not what you expected... but possible.

Leo and Libra (0.5/1): Constantly changing emotional states lead to initial exhilaration, often followed by exhaustion on the researcher's part. Lack of stability is made up for by shininess and willingness. Outcome of experiment difficult to predict, therefore the researcher may wish for more stable materials to work with.

Gemini (0.4/1): Comparable to positronium, an exotic matter-antimatter combination. Appealing as a potential source of tremendous energy, but likely to become explosively unstable under extensive probing. Wear safety goggles.

CONCLUSION:

Nothing in life is perfect, not even Love. Nonetheless, this knowledge does not make the issue go away. It is recommended that Virgos collect further data and reach their own conclusions in this regard.

True Tales of Heartbreak
The Libra Guide to **Compatibility**

You hear a lot that Libras are all about the romance because it's a Venus-ruled sign. I'm not sure that's entirely the point. I think most people are suckers for a good romance story, with all the twists and turns required for Boy to finally be with Girl. And Libras love the "love story" part of Love. That's probably why you find so many Libras who have an interest in astrology... it's like one of those "making of" documentaries on a romance movie DVD.

Here are the payoffs and pitfalls of Libras relationships with the other signs, expressed in terms those lovers of love will appreciate. Something that captures all the vibrancy and willful disregard for reality that Libras crave.... comic books!

ARIES: Pretty exciting stuff. Adventurous, motivated, and straight to the point. "Untamed" sounds pretty exciting, after all... until your untamed Aries wanders out of the yard to go chase something else. Your charm will catch Aries, but it may take continuous charm to keep Aries.

TAURUS: They love the lovin' just as much as you do... and who couldn't love that? The problem: is Taurus' considerable appetite for you, or is it just an appetite? And you love to be loved, but not necessarily possessed, and certainly not ordered around.

GEMINI: Charming. Witty. Fun. Affectionate. There will never be any doubt in your mind that Gemini loves you, except on the days his identical twin The Jerk shows up.

164

There he is lurking in the shadows now! Give it time... you'll be dating him too in time, and probably when you least expect it.

CANCER: Great depth of emotion. Tremendous power when in love. But when they cling to you... or when they think you're sneaking out to flirt with other boys... ouch! And that two headed monster Cancer is protecting you from? Odds are pretty good it's that most horrible of monsters: The Beast From Cancer's Jealous, Defensive Mind. All your ray guns may not be enough to stop it.

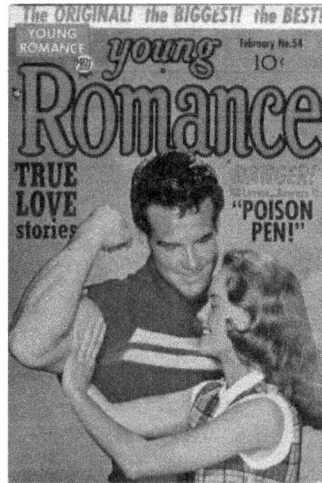

LEO: Great fun. Terribly romantic. Irresistibly kitty-cuddly-cute when they put their mind to it. Stroke their egos a little, and they're good to go. Just make sure you keep stroking... and stroking... and, hey, weren't there supposed to be two of us in this relationship?

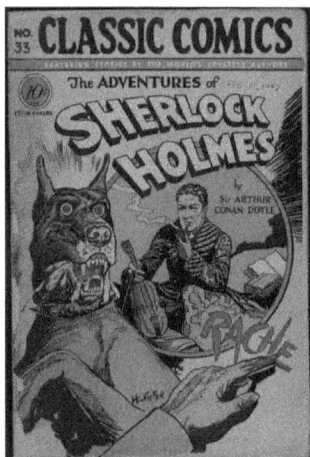

VIRGO: Admittedly they can be charming, and the things that logical little mind of theirs can come up with are adorable. But let's be honest: some days they just aren't that romantic at all. Unless of course you want a relationship based on word puzzles. Once you've found Virgo, you may have to keep searching to solve The Mystery Of The Missing Passion.

LIBRA: Okay, show of hands: how many of you out there can name a romance story you loved where two people who are completely different end up together anyway? Okay, now... how many of you can name a romance story you loved about two identical romantics who got together, everything was just great, and they spent the rest of their lives that way? Yeah, thought so. Romance is as much about the differences as it is about the similarities.

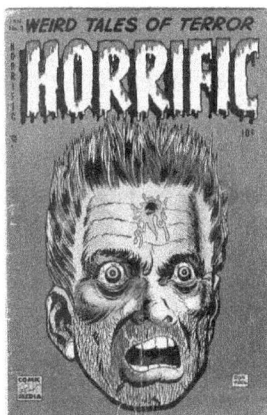

SCORPIO: Such passion! Such intensity! Such intrigue! Such a shame that they tend to see everything as something to be dissected, exposed, and dragged into the light of day (or back under their rock to be eaten). These relationships usually start out sexy and end up as just a mess of fluids, and all the forensics in the world may not help you make sense of it.

SAGITTARIUS: They're a lot of fun. They know how to have a good time. You'll like the playfulness. Before long, the combination of childlike delight and deep philosophical interaction and passion will have you thinking "marriage." And – what's this? "Dear Libra: You're great babe but I gotta move on. Strange new worlds to explore and all that. Yours truly, Sagittarius..."

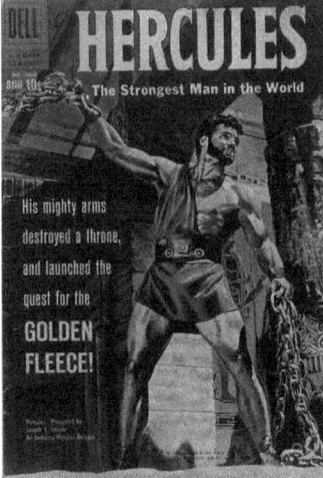

Capricorn: He's capable, he knows what he's doing, and he sure looks like a good deal. That kind of focus could really make you feel special, and could really

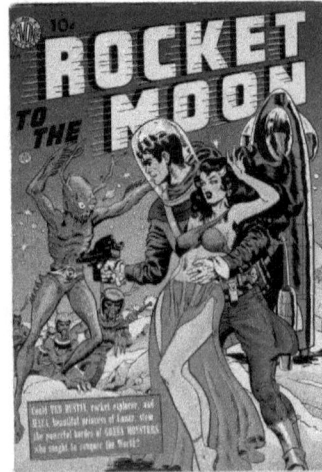

make a relationship take flight. But, wait a minute... he's off strangling a lion with his bare hands today. Maybe tomorrow he'll be romantic. Oh wait, tomorrow he's scheduled to slay a monster. And he isn't going to alter his schedule for anything. Including you.

Aquarius: He's interesting, intelligent, and different. There's a sense that life with Aquarius could be a non-stop thrill ride of action and adventure and romance. Sure, it could turn out that way. The problem here is that he's on his own world half the time... not yours.

Pices: What started out as a refreshing dip into the deep waters of Lake Dewey-Eyes can quickly turn into being surrounded by weird, creepy things that don't even breathe the same way you do. Or breathe at all for that matter. And believe me... on a bad day, you'll want to come up for air.

WE DARE YOU TO TAKE THESE
Adventures into
DARKNESS
-FROZEN DEATH

CSI: Romance
The Scorpio Guide To Compatibility

There's a mystery to be uncovered here. A blow to the heart... an intense, passionate experience causing shortness of breath, rapid irregular heartbeat, and a flood of endorphins throughout the nervous system, clouding judgement. Although it's enticing, you can sense the ever-present spectre of danger... and that only increases your curiosity. Congratulations! You're a Scorpio in a relationship! Here's what you can expect...

*** *Scene: The Las Vegas Coroner's Autopsy Room. Chief Investigator Gil Grissom and coroner Dr. Al Robbins stand over the badly-mangled body of an adult male.*

DOC: Victim was a white male, approximately 35 years old, name unknown. A Scorpio.

GRISSOM: How can you tell?

DOC: We found this medallion on the victim. Also, this scorpion tattoo. Scorpios love that stuff. There's little sign of struggle... we can presume the victim knew his assailant. Probably someone he was in a relationship with.

GRISSOM: A **Taurus**?

AL: That's a common guess... but notice the large chest wound. Tauruses are steady and sensual, which would explain the relationship, but their killing technique is usually through stubbornness... refusal to budge.

GRISSOM: Another Water Sign, maybe?

AL: Good possibility of it. They have the emotional depth a Scorpio is looking for. But I'd expect the body to be more weighed down with the assailant's emotional baggage if it was a **Cancer**, and there's no mawkish sentiment filling the lungs, so it wasn't the usual Pisces drowning.

GRISSOM: It could have been a **Capricorn**.

AL: Yes. Scorpio's seem to find them sexy, but there's limited bruising here. Capricorn usually kill their partners by battering them to death with their inflexibility. Like Taurus, only edgier.

GRISSOM: An **Aries**, maybe? They're both Mars-ruled, they both love excitement...

AL: And Aries doesn't usually have the patience for Scorpio's caution and analysis. Although admittedly, the passion and potential violence of Aries and Scorpio together is noteworthy.

GRISSOM: It could have been another **Scorpio**.

AL: I doubt it. They cling on to each other passionately enough, but Scorpios usually bury their flaws... and their victims... deep enough for no one to find them until it's too late. This guy was found on his couch. Notice the tissue under the victim's fingernails: it matches the scarring around the ears. It's self-inflicted.

GRISSOM: Like he was trying to claw out his own eardrums. Maybe a **Gemini or a Virgo**, then. Scorpio's love watching the thought processes those two have, until the talking has gone on too long.

AL: Good point. But I'm not sure a relationship with a Gemini would have the depth our vic was looking for, and the vic's eardrums aren't swollen from the debating. I did a swab of the genitals... no recent sign of sexual activity. Scorpios usually go ape for Virgos that way. Death by nagging *is* the Virgo style, though.

GRISSOM: **Sagittarius? Libra?**

AL: They both have their charms, but I'm not sure either one has the depth Scorpio is looking for. At least they don't usually act like it enough to Scorpio's liking. No glucose poisoning, which is Libra's usual *m.o.*, and no hoof marks from a Sagittarius stampeding away, which they usually do quickly.

GRISSOM: I suppose the logical place to look then would be with Scorpio's least compatible signs... **Leo and Aquarius.**

AL: Aquarius is usually too hard to pin down for a Scorpio... which can be intriguing, but Aquarians don't usually kill off their victims so dramatically. They prefer to remove their partners through diffusion in abstract thought processes. A Leo certainly has the passion a Scorpio wants, but the Leo usually kills via self-importance and/or pomposity. I dusted for pomposity... none present.

(*CSI agent SARAH SIDLE enters, waving a note*)

SARAH: Gris, we found this note at the crime scene!

GRIS: You mean...?

SARAH: *He did it to himself!*

GRIS: We usually do, Sarah. We usually do.

They're Off And Running!
The Sagittarius Guide To Compatibility

Sagittarians are always being accused of treating their love lives as if they were a sporting event, rather than like love lives. And why not? There's anticipation, competition, and... more often than not... someone loses. So in that spirit, here's the handy Sagittarius race card for who's in the running, with odds of a win. No horse in this race is a guaranteed winner, but some bets are a lot safer than others. Then again, no guts, no glory...

Here are today's odds on a winning relationship for you, Sag:

Aries and Leo (3:2 odds): A fairly safe bet. Popular favourites, both these Fire signs have the sport you require. You may find Aries is awfully hard to steer into the chute, and Leo is sometimes more interested in being a show pony than a race winner.

Gemini (3:1 odds): Quick, responsive, and sporty... much like you. This is a pairing that often has people saying "oh gosh, you two are perfect for each other!" The problem is that despite the horseplay, deep down you have a thick, chewy philosophical center. You may never get past the sneaking suspicion that, with Gemini, it's question marks all the way down...

Libra and Aquarius (4:1 odds): Both good bets, overall, with proven records of performance. Generally pleasant to get along with. Libra sometimes has a preference for standing there are just looking pretty when the bell rings. Aquarius is a bit of a rebel and you like that... but sometimes it's hard to figure out what they're rebelling against. It may be *you.*

Virgo and Pisces (5:1 odds): Both unusual choices: the squares to one's own sign aren't where you usually look for a safe relationship bet. But both of these tend to outperform in long muddy stretches, compared to their reputations. Who knows why? You probably just love the challenge. Pisces is sometimes lacking the horse sense you require in a mate, and Virgo on a bad day? Nag, nag, nag...

Taurus (6:1 odds): A bull... not a horse. This can lend a lot of stability to a relationship... something Sagittarius usual forgets to bring to the table. Pleasant and generally kind... but if you were expecting to saddle up a Bull and get anywhere quickly... you're in the wrong race, pal.

Cancer (8:1 odds): Jupiter rules Sagittarius, and is exalted in Cancer. Theoretically, this should make for great mutual joy and a solid philosophical relationship. The problem here is that crabs are designed to withstand accidental trampling... but they're always waiting for it too. And you'll provide it... probably by accident. So long, Crab.

Sagittarius (9:1 odds)

SAG 1: I'm having a great time!

SAG 2: Me too! Did you remember to bring the stability?

SAG 1: No dude, I thought you had that covered.

SAG 2: And, damn, we're outta beer.

SAG 1: It's okay, I'll go to the store and get more.

SAG 2: You aren't coming back, are you?

SAG 1: Probably not.

SAG 2: Okay. Later, dude...

Capricorn (10:1 odds): Obstinate, stubborn, and although they can have a fiery temperament, that fire doesn't seem to be fuelling anything visible, a lot of the time. They can provide a valuable stabilizing, steering force in your life. Do you need that? Hell yeah! Do you like that? If your answer is "yes," it's time for the veterinarian to cut back on your tranquilizers.

Scorpio (15:1 odds): They have all the intensity and focus you lack. Of course, you never really asked for intensity and focus. or you did, and it just isn't your style. They like sex though, and you do too. A sure winner... provided all the other horses break their legs first, and Scorpio doesn't break yours.

Oh, and one more thing, Sagittarius? You've already got a bad enough reputation for running around on your relationships. Don't go betting on the trifecta, okay?

Your Attention Please
The Capricorn Guide to Compatibility

Comrades:

Certain forces have conspired to, at times, deny Capricorn the love and romance that Capricorn requires to function as a powerful, independent entity. In order to more efficiently address this matter, you have all been assigned to one of twelve cadres. You will receive your final score when you return home, or to the factory, or to Re-Education Camp, where you will have a glorious time supporting our future triumph over the forces of solitude.

Aries: Your fire and passion are admirable, but it's so uncontrolled and undisciplined that there's a constant risk of you burning down what we've built. Go to the camp.

Taurus: Solid, dependable worker. Excellent at following the Party Line, but your focus on the comforts of life... including a slight tendency to stray... is worrisome. You may return to your home.

Gemini: Scattered. I have a hard time believing that you believe in the goals of The Party, given your fondness for enemy propaganda. Your charm is lovely, but it also makes me suspicious. Report to Camp!

Cancer: Sweet, moody, and defensive, just like me. With time and discipline, you could make Chairman. Just watch the overreacting with distance when I overreact to you with distance. Report to home.... and bake me cookies.

Leo: Completely counter-revolutionary. I understand the need to keep the troops entertained, but I always feel like the Andrews Sisters are still on stage with you when it's time to charge the enemy hill instead. You know where we could use talent like that? *Camp!*

Virgo: Excellent quality. Stable, intelligent, and efficient. However, you tendency to worry is worrisome to me, and makes me question your loyalty. But I know you don't mean it. Return home anyway, with an escort from Security.

Libra: Decadent! Completely unfocused on anything of real value to The Party. All this romance and sweetness is merely a cover for your desire to not take things seriously. The appearance of not taking it seriously enough is equivalent to lack of seriousness. *Thoughtcrime!* Report to Camp!

Scorpio: I admire your intensity, and how well-armed you are. That intensity can be worrisome though: it makes you prone to lashing out. A little time in the factory sewing cheap exports will perfect you. Once you've learned you're lesson... full parole.

Sagittarius: Once again, entertainment value is no substitute for ideological commitment. You have ideology certainly... it just isn't *mine*. And what you *do* have is shamefully disorganized. Thank you for the attempt at amusement. *Camp!*

Capricorn: Solid and dependable, just like me. Secretly sweet too... just like me. Truly an equal. The only problem here: do you recall being told this was a *democracy*? No, neither do I. Allow me to demonstrate. Go to the factory!

Aquarius: We're so completely different that it's hard to see how you can fit into the society I have planned for you. But you're dedicated to a higher goal too, so you may report to the factory. But sit right under Surveillance Camera Twelve.

Pisces: Your emotionality isn't my usual style, but this foreign technology called "compassion" you possess is of great interest to The Party. In time, it could be forged into a powerful weapon of romantic victory. Report to home, and stand by for further compliance.

There will now be a fifteen-minute period of romantic exchanges. You are instructed to enjoy this.

This Is Not The Aquarius Guide To Compatibility

Dear Aquarius:

As you may have noticed, I've been doing a series on how the signs perform in their relationships with other signs. People seem to like this sort of thing, and admittedly relationship issues are the one thing I come across most often in the course of my profession. I have to admit, though: I was a little stumped as to what kind of approach to take with Aquarius. Frankly, I'm not the only one, as you may have noticed yourself.

An Aquarius is born with the knowledge (on some level) that the individual differences between us are like different songs playing on different radio stations at the same time. Even though you can only listen to one station at a time, you (above all others) realize that the same air is being pierced by hundreds of signals at hundreds of frequencies... each one carrying unique sounds. You are born *knowing* that, whereas most of the rest of us never even catch on that such a thing is happening all around us, all the time.

You have the same heart and feelings that everyone else does. The problem isn't *you*, in a sense: it's *everyone else*. Have you ever read what they say about you? That's you're so aloof and weird that it's hard to make a relationship work with you? What a load of crap. The big problem anyone has with a relationship with an Aquarius is that the others aren't used to listening to all those higher frequencies, literally or figuratively, like you were born to do.

Find a way to explain that to your partner in a language they understand, and all will be well.

Sure, I could give you the quick and dirty lowdown on how this man or that woman works with you. If I did, it would look kind of like this...

Aries: Fun but not always dependable or stable for you.

Taurus: Dependable and stable but sometimes not that much fun for you.

Gemini: Intellectually interesting but emotionally scattered. At least, by your standards.

Cancer: Emotionally interesting but intellectually scattered. At least, by your standards.

Leo: Fun, but wants to fight you for top billing. At least, by your standards.

Virgo: Caring but a little too conventional. At least, by your standards.

Libra: Sweet but unchallenging, or too challenging in their refusal to challenge you. At least, by your standards.

Scorpio: Emotionally intense, but doesn't know when to detach. At least, by your standards.

Sagittarius: A fun partner, but goes off on different tangents than yours. At least, by your standards.

Capricorn: Has emotional depth, but has a different game plan laid out than you do. At least, by your standards.

Aquarius: Beats the hell outta me! And that's by *anyone's* standards.

Pisces: Pleasantly mushy, yet unpleasantly mushy. At least, by your standards.

...and I could ornament it with some jokes and a funny picture, and we'd all have a good laugh. But none of that would actually address why you've come looking for a compatibility guide, would it? I suggest being Aquarian with this, and leap to the conclusion the rest of us would struggle a little longer to make: if you have a problem with *X*, go read *X*'s entry in this series.

So: Let the Cancers and the Virgos and the Aries and such have their compatibility guides. Me? I'd rather give you something new and unique that you could really use.

Would you like a hug?

Goldilocks And The Twelve Signs: The Pisces Guide To Compatibility

Once upon a time Goldilocks went to Speed Dating, sponsored by the National Oat Growers Association... so naturally porridge was involved. She sat down at the big, long table and prepared to receive her potential suitors.

Before anyone else had a chance to sit down, **Aries** zipped in and filled the chair in front of her. "Hey baby," Aries said, "try mine first!" Goldilocks tried his porridge. It intrigued her, but the flavor impulsively faded before she could really get into it. So she decided to wait for the next suitor.

Taurus came next. His porridge was smooth and comforting and sensual, and she really liked it. But then Taurus criticized her spoon technique, calling it ungrounded. This miffed Goldilocks to no end, especially when Taurus called her "ungrounded."

Then **Gemini** sat down. Gemini's porridge was full of interesting flavor combinations, any one of which would have been fine on its own, but the saffron and marjoram covered up the comfort and warmth she was really seeking.

Cancer offered his bowl next. Goldilocks was intrigued by the depth of feeling Cancer put into his offering. The conversation went well, and Goldilocks suggested they meet again; But Cancer became too defensive and scurried off.

Leo came next. His bowl was hot and shiny and flavorful... as appealing as Cancer's, but more adventurous. But then Leo started telling her in detail how she was enjoying the wrong flavors, and how she didn't appreciate his technique, and moved on, flipping his hair as he left.

Virgo sat down and offered his porridge. It was delicious. "Why do you think so?" Virgo asked. Then Virgo asked what basis for comparison Goldilocks had, her experience with porridge, and the exact mileage to her home. Goldilocks felt interrogated and over analyzed, so she ran out the clock with Virgo by discussing her health issues.

Libra sat down and handed over his porridge. It was smooth and sweet and Pisces really enjoyed it. Then Libra began to question why Goldilocks thought so, and why Goldilocks picked that outfit to wear today, then accused Goldilocks of being evasive when she couldn't answer the questions adequately.

Scorpio came next and offered his bowl. It was intense and affectionate and exactly what Goldilocks was looking for. Everything was going great until Goldilocks accidentally called Scorpio "Cancer." Scorpio sat up straight and spent the remainder of his time berating Pisces for being unfaithful and criticizing Goldilocks' taste in foot wear.

Sagittarius came next. His porridge was warm and exciting, with an adventurous dash of curry. Once she finished, Goldilocks looked up from her bowl to ask for more, only to discover that Sagittarius had wandered off into the wine tasting next door, and was hitting on an ad executive from Cleveland.

Capricorn sat down and Goldilocks tried his porridge next. It was hearty and filling and good. Goldilocks asked Capricorn if she could see him again. By the time Capricorn finished delineating the cost of his porridge's ingredients, the time involved to make it, and how his portfolio was performing, Goldilocks had lost interest and felt a little sad.

Aquarius sat down and offered his bowl of porridge. His bowl was interesting and unique, and Goldilocks found it intriguing. Unfortunately, Aquarius didn't provide a spoon, so Goldilocks was unable to get into it in any real depth. The surface looked interesting, though. They spent the rest of their time staring at each other and then out the window.

Finally, **Pisces** sat down. Goldilocks was a Pisces too. This naturally started up a long conversation about their childhood dreams, last week's episode of Grey's Anatomy, and where the best place to get married would be. Unfortunately, when it came to setting up a second date, Pisces was just as scattered as Goldilocks, and nothing came of it.

Goldilocks stared out the window sadly. It had started to rain. Maybe she should just give up on the whole idea of ever finding someone whose porridge gave her the combination of strength, sensitivity, and romance that she was hungry for.

Just as she got up to leave, Aries zipped in and filled the chair in front of her. "Hey baby," Aries said...